New Testament
Books
and Te

DATE DUE		

New Testament Books for Pastor and Teacher

RALPH P. MARTIN

THE WESTMINSTER PRESS
Philadelphia

Book Design by Alice Derr

First edition

Published by The Westminster Press₍ₑₓₜ₎
Philadelphia, Pennsylvania

PRINTED IN THE UNITED STATES OF AMERICA
9 8 7 6 5 4 3 2 1

Library of Congress Cataloging in Publication Data

Martin, Ralph P.
New Testament books for pastor and teacher.

Bibliography: p.
Includes index.
1. Bible. N.T.—Bibliography. I. Title.
Z7772.L1M3 1984   016.225   83-21654
[BS2330.2]
ISBN 0-664-24511-0 (pbk.)

Contents

Abbreviations

AB	The Anchor Bible
CGTC	Cambridge Greek Testament Commentary
CNT	Commentaire du Nouveau Testament
EB	Etudes Bibliques
EKK	Evangelisch-katholischer Kommentar
E.T.	English Translation
HNTC	Harper's New Testament Commentaries (published in Britain as Black's New Testament Commentaries)
HTKNT	Herders Theologischer Kommentar zum Neuen Testament
HzNT	Handbuch zum Neuen Testament
IB	*The Interpreter's Bible*
ICC	International Critical Commentary
ISBE	*International Standard Bible Encyclopedia*
MeyerK	Meyer Kommentar
MNTC	Moffatt New Testament Commentary
NCB	New Century Bible
n.d.	No date given
NICNT	New International Commentary on the New Testament (published in Britain as the New London Commentary on the New Testament)
NIDNTT	*New International Dictionary of New Testament Theology*
NIGTC	New International Greek Testament Commentary

NTD	Das Neue Testament Deutsch
RGG	*Die Religion in Geschichte und Gegenwart*
SB	Sources Bibliques
SNTS	Society for New Testament Studies
THKNT	Theologischer Handkommentar zum Neuen Testament
TNTC	Tyndale New Testament Commentary
WBC	Word Biblical Commentary
ZBKNT	Zürcher Bibelkommentar zum Neuen Testament

Preface

The assignment to put together the contents of this little book has been found both easy and difficult. The paradox is resolved by my explaining that I have had an excellent model to follow; hence the task has been simplified in advance and its contours already drawn, waiting only to be filled in.

Professor Brevard S. Childs's book on Old Testament resources published as *Old Testament Books for Pastor and Teacher* has proved a strength and a stimulus, and inevitably our judgments on some common titles have overlapped. Where I have differed from him in assessing a particular title that covers both Old and New Testaments, I have done so with diffidence and respect. So many students, ministers, and teachers have paid rightful tribute to the worth and usefulness of his book that it has been a daunting enterprise to try to follow in its clearly marked steps.

But my encountering difficulty refers also to another side of this task. Nothing is so individualistic as recommending books, since tastes, interests, and criteria all differ from one person to another. I have found myself passing a negative opinion on a book that some readers, I am sure, will have found profitable at some point in their life. Conversely, a few of my selections rescue from an undeserved oblivion some titles that others may judge of little value or may have dismissed for several reasons. Making value judgments is a risky business, however, and often not very profitable. The philosopher George in Tom Stoppard's play *Jumpers* comments on the absurdity of analyzing the statement, "This is a good bacon sandwich." It may be just as well, therefore, if I say something here about the principles that have informed my choices.

I share Childs's enthusiasm for seeing the authority of Scripture as canon firmly established among the church's pastors and teachers, and I believe with him that the recovery of "expository preaching"—always controlled by the requirements of its relevance and its application to a wide agenda of personal and social concerns—is one of the great desirables in the churches today. Theological colleges and seminaries have a vital part to play in securing this end. So while I have kept the parish minister's task foremost in my sights, at the same time an eye has been open to the needs of teachers, in both church and theological school, who have the interests of tomorrow's ministers at heart and seek to prepare them for their pastoral tasks.

The recommendations cover several parts of New Testament study, with priority given to commentaries that elucidate the text. I have always felt that in building up a minister's library the first claim on limited resources should be directed to collecting commentaries as the most serviceable and enduring investment possible. Harold H. Rowley told his students at Manchester that, even when his family budget was limited, his wife agreed that his purchase of books would be their first priority. That may now seem to most ministers an idealistic arrangement, but the story is worth remembering, especially as Rowley's library grew to become a legend and his bibliographical control was phenomenal.

Books in the English language obviously are the main choices, but occasionally an exceptional work in German or French has been noted. But choices are not restricted to these commentary volumes, however important they are, and however deserving of first claim on the pastor's book allowance. Several study books that I have personally found illuminating and helpful have been included, and I have constantly been reaching back into my memory to recall the ten years spent as a minister in pastoral work before entering on a teaching vocation at the university and seminary level. Also my lists reflect books that are either currently in print or available in most good libraries, whether university or public. I have not been able to share Childs's penchant for valued titles now centuries old, and I would justify this limitation on the ground that *good* modern commentaries—at least in my experience—build on the wisdom and insights of their predecessors and incorporate much of lasting worth that the Puritan, Reformed, and orthodox divines bequeathed to us. Besides, I am a pragmatist in recognizing that a busy pastor, as distinct from the student and scholar, needs recommendations that are manageable and utilitarian. I trust that this is a realistic appraisal and applies also to teachers in our day when administrative chores, committee work, counseling of students, and denominational responsibilities eat into so much study time.

To be sure, this delimiting of scope does not mean that I disdain the past. Rather, I have found—in company with many others for whom Childs speaks—much uplift and inspiration in (for example) Calvin's commentaries, Luther on *Romans*, and Wesley's *Notes*, to say nothing of lesser authors such as Joseph Addison Alexander, *The Gospel According to Matthew* (1860), on chs. 1–16; Thomas Manton, *James* (1693); and William Gurnall, *The Christian in Complete Armour* (1655), on Ephesians 6. These classics are well known, and I have taken as much for granted.

One of the saddest experiences is to talk to ministerial groups where one's fellow ministers frankly confess that they have no time or energy for study. The pressures of life in a busy world make these admissions understandable but hardly excusable. We usually can make time for what we really want to do. I hope that these reading lists will not appear too threatening, but rather that they may excite some readers to reorder their lives to make room for that essential task, namely, the reflective study of New Testament Scripture as part of a person's readiness for ministry. The titles have been selected with a view to encouraging pastors and teachers at the place where they are.

Another guideline I have followed is to pick out only those titles of which I have personal knowledge. My recommendations are made strictly on the basis of a "hands-on" experience (as they say in the high-tech industry) and represent what has been of value to me in both ministry and teaching. It would have been relatively easy to comb the lists of published titles and quote at random. Having to restrict oneself to books of proven worth is another matter, and the selection reflects the limitations and proclivities of the present writer, as well as his opportunities.

This book joins its partner in the shared hope that it may be a not unworthy companion volume, awakening fresh interest in the New Testament as the church's book and God's word written for our learning, proclamation, and teaching.

It is only fitting to pay a tribute to the secretarial help of Evelyn F. Dugan and Janet M. Gathright; and to the bibliographical help provided by Lynn A. Losie and Erwin Penner, who, along with Janet Gathright, are currently students in the doctoral studies program.

R.P.M.

Fuller Theological Seminary
Pasadena, California

I
Aim
and Approach

The avowed intention of these chapters is to offer some guidance in the selection and use of books that can help the reader understand and communicate the message of the New Testament documents. The person most likely to need this kind of help will be the working minister, to whom is given the great privilege and awesome responsibility of being a servant of the word to his or her people.

The role of the pastor as preacher and teacher is one that has fallen on bad times. People, we are told, no longer attend church to hear sermons and are distrustful of the pastor whose chief credentials are a facility with words and a pulpit presence. Other aspects of the ministerial calling are reckoned to be more desirable and important. The pastor should be an efficient and creative organizer, an expert and sympathetic counselor, and a warmhearted individual, good at relating to people and their situations. What one does in the service of worship and how one performs in the pulpit are less highly regarded. Or so it has seemed in our generation.

There are signs, however, that the attitude of congregations is changing. In particular, they are becoming more demanding and they expect that the hour of worship should be more thoughtfully planned and prepared for.

Also, the sermon is reasserting its central role in the liturgy, both Catholic and Reformed. The Constitution on the Sacred Liturgy, which came out of Vatican II, made this point, and worshipers have not been slow to respond:

The ministry of preaching is to be fulfilled most faithfully and carefully. The sermon, moreover, should draw its content mainly from scriptural and liturgical sources, for it is the proclamation of God's wonderful works in the history of salvation, which is the mystery of Christ ever made present and active in us.

Protestant believers who look back to the Continental Reformers as their founding fathers really should need no further encouragement to give the sermon a place of high dignity. There are signs too that as part of the renewal of worship in free churches the "ministry of the word" is again recovering its place as the chosen medium by which God speaks and gives himself to his gathered people. Taught by such perceptive prophets as P. T. Forsyth and Karl Barth, a new generation of ordained ministers are viewing seriously their office as "servants of the divine word." They are coming to see that the sermon—"the word of God in the words of men and women"—stands in a middle position between the age-old purpose of God in salvation history and the present-day needs, aspirations, and ambitions of the people of God. The several ways in which the divine will impinges on human activity—personal, social, national, and worldwide—are the agenda items of Christian preachers as they come before the congregation with that unique utterance called "the sermon."

And the sermon, to be true to its name, must be rooted in the scriptural soil of God's written word. Hence the aspiring prophet will be above all a student of that word. Thus one will value as precious beyond price the hours spent in the study wrestling to hear God unfold his mind through words that, though written ages ago, have perennial appeal and timeless authority.

Because the present writer believes that the day of the sermon is not over and never will be, he has tried to direct what he has to recommend primarily to pastors but also to teachers called to shape and stimulate the thinking of Christian students, especially those in training for the church's ministry in its manifold variety. The present writer, like Professor Childs, has no reluctance in adopting a confessional stance. Obviously no denominational or ecclesiastical bias is intended in this admission; and the impression should not be given (and I trust it will not be received as the book is read) that the author has in view only a particular type of minister or student. The term "confessional" implies, rather, that New Testament study is of special relevance and significance to those who stand within the household of Christian faith. But this conviction should not be interpreted in any narrow sectarian or exclusive sense.

One more guideline in the choice of titles ought to be recognized at the outset. The New Testament as a body of ancient literature may be approached along many routes. The student of Greco-Roman society has interests that are served by studying these ancient documents. Those involved in a recent phase of New Testament research have been asking pertinent questions about the social history and corporate identity of Christian groups as illumined by these books. In a previous generation the History of Religions school opened up a new field of inquiry by seeking to plot the New Testament documents in the wider framework of Hellenistic religious culture. Yet again, the proposal of a liturgical origin of the New Testament literature correctly pointed to the first use of Gospels and epistles in the worshiping life of those faraway congregations. What we read today initially saw the light of day in a context of public assembly. The New Testament can therefore be best appreciated if it is kept closely tied to the church's offices of prayer and proclamation. The present writer has the greatest sympathy with the last-named suggestion.

At the same time the New Testament, as an assortment of twenty-seven books, has a setting other than the university classroom and the church's sanctuary, though we recognize a legitimacy in both of these contexts. The New Testament in its canonical shape (as it later came to be known) has always been granted the character of a word of God and seen as the

repository of Christian belief and practice. This feature stems
from the role of New Testament Scripture as an evangelistic
tool and an agent of mission as God has been pleased to
extend his rule over human lives in the planting and nurturing
of new congregations. From one angle this characterization of
the New Testament as *the book of the Christian mission* means
that its primary focus is God, who is at work in his world just
as he became incarnate in his only Son, and who continues his
gracious presence by the Holy Spirit living in the congregation. We recommend therefore a simple criterion: Books
about the New Testament that pay respect to its chief theme
and function as the record of God's activity in Jesus Christ for
the reconciliation and remaking of the world are most likely
to speak directly to the preacher's needs, given that his or her
task, directly or indirectly, lies exactly in this ongoing enterprise of Christian mission.

One other dimension is worth mentioning. History has
declared that while Christianity arose as a religious movement
and social phenomenon in the eastern Mediterranean basin,
its faith became most signally understood, articulated, and
expressed in Western Europe and later in the New World of
the North American continent. The reading lists that follow
reflect that debt, since the author knows only that tradition.
At the same time he recognizes the wealth that lies, largely
inaccessible to Western eyes, in the Orthodox and Eastern
churches. And he would be foolish to deny that the future of
Christian thought and the interpretation of the New Testament in particular may well be bound up with the churches of
the southern hemisphere or, more particularly, those of the
emerging nations of Latin America, Africa, and the Orient.
Often, however, it is church leaders of today in those areas
who wish to know how best to lay a foundation on which they
can build their thinking and fashion it according to their own
cultural milieu and its opportunities. The writer has had such
requests in mind while drawing on the only resources he has
known firsthand, in his own experience and knowledge as
student, pastor, and teacher.

II
Bibliographies
in General

In the main, guides that set out to select and recommend books, or that merely list book titles, across the entire spectrum of the theological encyclopedia are too thin for our purpose. And they range in scope, stance, and utility from *The Minister's Library,* by Cyril J. Barber, to *The Reader's Guide to the Best Evangelical Books,* edited by Mark L. Branson. Both works have some good features. Barber supplies in most cases a thumbnail assessment of each title and picks up some older works, but his judgments are essentially limited by an extreme right-wing conservative position, and his survey is dated. We understand that a second volume to update the entries is in progress and is due to appear shortly. If the first volume is reprinted, a fair number of factual errors will need correcting. Branson's handbook, on the other hand, is up-to-date (1982) and ranges over the full extent of Christian literature. Less than fifty pages are occupied with New Testament matters, but they contain some pithy assessments of mainly recent publications, with larger evaluations of books judged to be significant on the current scene. The criteria used in assessing these books are not always clear, but it is evident that the presence of a concern for social and ethical questions is always given high marks and its absence leads to a negative evaluation. Whether this discrimination is fair may be questioned, however. The theological stance is pleasingly "open," and this manual should have a wider appeal than its own title implies.

Useful, but of less value for our enterprise are John Bollier's *The Literature of Theology: A Guide for Students and Pastors;* William J. Grier, *The Best Books: A Guide to Christian Literature* (extremely conservative in its orientation); and John B. Trotti (ed.), *Aids to a Theological Library.*

David M. Scholer's *A Basic Bibliographic Guide for New Testament Exegesis* is directed more to the student than to the minister, but its pages are always worth consulting as a checklist. Critical comments are kept at a minimum, usually only a few words.

A more constructive compilation of New Testament commentary titles was prepared by Anthony C. Thiselton for the journal *The Theological Students' Fellowship Bulletin,* 1970; it was revised by Donald A. Carson and issued separately in 1977. Thiselton's observations are worth pondering.

I have personally gained as much help from the periodicals that carry, on a regular basis, surveys of current New Testament literature and especially commentaries. Three or four of the more obscure journals are not generally known to ministers. These are accessible only in fairly large libraries, and that fact may prove a hindrance. I refer to the *Internationale Zeitschriftenschau für Bibelwissenschaft und Grenzgebiete,* with entries usually written in German, sometimes French and English, which gives a paragraph of summary of new books and even significant essays appearing in journals; and the *Elenchus Bibliographicus Biblicus,* which has appeared regularly since 1920 (in the Catholic journal *Biblica* until 1968, and separately since then). It lists only titles and gives no data on content. *New Testament Abstracts* does a slightly fuller and equally invaluable job of reporting and summarizing new books and journal articles on the New Testament text, its background, world, and theology. The abstracts are written in English. For a verse-by-verse listing of journal articles and books, *An Exegetical Bibliography of the New Testament,* edited by Günter Wagner at the Baptist Theological Seminary, Rüschlikon-Zürich, Switzerland, is a monumental project and is continuing. This work should be of great assistance to teachers wishing to be well informed on past research.

More easily obtainable are two semipopular but immensely rewarding journals that every pastor ought to read: *The Expository Times,* published in Edinburgh, and *Interpretation: A Journal of Bible and Theology,* a product of Union Theological Seminary, Richmond, Virginia. Both journals expressly cater to the working pastor and student but at a high level that challenges one's thinking as well as informing it. *The Expository Times* regularly features articles on the best commentaries in current use or on recent trends in biblical studies. These essays, written by leading international scholars, are of special value in helping us to catch up on our reading and keep abreast of scholarship. *Interpretation* is no less informative with its systematic offering of essays on particular biblical books and themes, and it can even devote an issue to the question of what to look for in a commentary (*Interpretation* 36:4 [1982]). The essays in this issue might well be read alongside the present book, in particular the practical tips on commentary buying given by Edgar Krentz (pp. 380–381). In a close second place, offering help in preparing sermons on a given New Testament Gospel or epistle, is the Southern Baptist Theological Seminary's publication, *Review and Expositor,* which features helpful essays by faculty and ministers to correspond with the Convention's chosen biblical book to be used in the churches.

We turn now to consider some standard guides for the task of exegeting the New Testament as Scripture.

III
Basic
Exegetical Tools

Frederick W. Danker's *Multipurpose Tools for Bible Study* heads the list of bibliographical guides, as it does in Brevard Childs's *Old Testament Books for Pastor and Teacher.* The single complaint I have is an inevitable one. Even Danker's third edition of 1970 is quickly becoming dated, and several of his chapters need enriching and updating, excellent as they were when first published. The areas where strengthening is required are noted below.

Help is at hand in two publications of the Inter-Varsity Press. The first of these, *A Bibliographical Guide to New Testament Research*, edited by Richard T. France, has now appeared in a third edition (1979), published by the Journal for the Study of the Old Testament, at the University of Sheffield, England. Earlier editions (1968 and 1974) were released under the auspices of the Tyndale Fellowship for Biblical Research in Cambridge, England. The latest edition contains the fullest bibliographical listing of exegetical helps currently in print. It is oriented to the British scene, but without too much difficulty one can match American editions to their British counterparts.

This guidebook ranges over the widest areas possible, from library aids and standard periodical titles to the more exotic fields of investigation such as papyrology, Qumran and the inter-Testamental period, and early Christian and Gnostic literature. It even gives tips about learning a modern language such as German or French as a means of access to so much that is being written by leading theologians in our day. Inevitably there are blind spots, and American readers would have appreciated more on the Nag Hammadi texts and the Jewish noncanonical literature that Scholars Press is making available in edited translations. See George W. E. Nickelsburg, *Jewish Literature between the Bible and the Mishnah*, for details as to existing and forthcoming editions in this field.

The second publication is more replete with important data, conveniently brought together in a manageable booklet. *Jesus and the Synoptic Gospels*, edited by David E. Aune, is the first in a series of Theological Students' Fellowship—Institute for Biblical Research study guides. Its excellent, encyclopedic coverage of titles that can be sought in the limited area of Jesus and the first three Gospels is only part of the book's usefulness. Methods of criticism and reviews of research are judiciously examined. Linguistic studies on the Gospels are scrutinized. Then the contemporary world of Judaism is treated before the various phases of Jesus' earthly life and ministry are referred to, each section covering what Aune believes to be the best guides available, both books and periodical essays. Students will find these resources invaluable, but alert pastors cannot fail to profit if they will take Aune's little book along on their next excursion to a seminary or public library.

In briefer compass there is Joseph A. Fitzmyer's *An Introductory Bibliography for the Study of Scripture* (rev. ed., 1981). In a few pages this handbook tells us all we need to know about current journals, lexicons, grammars, concordances, and Bible dictionaries, as well as summarizing in a few judicious sentences what to expect from New Testament theologies and commentary series. A most useful book to have on hand.

All would-be expositors of the sacred text will need an up-to-date Greek New Testament, which should lie open on their study desk or table. The larger the Greek font used the better, for ease of reference. The "best" is Nestle-Aland, *Novum Testamentum Graece*, in its 26th edition (1979). There is a pocket-size edition, but I recommend the larger, wide-margin edition to students and newly ordained ministers. It will be the investment of a lifetime. I have used the British and Foreign Bible Society edition in a wide-margin text for two decades now, and I wish I had been advised to get a similar edition years before. Most seminary students seem to incline to *The Greek New Testament*, ed. by Kurt Aland, Matthew Black, Carlo M. Martini, Bruce M. Metzger, and Allen Wikgren, in the United Bible Societies' third edition of 1975, which has an up-to-date text and is easier to read than Nestle. The critical apparatus gives fewer variant readings, but with fuller references. A companion volume, edited by Bruce M. Metzger, *A Textual Commentary on the Greek New Testament*, is most useful in giving the principles on which choices were made in producing the United Bible Societies' text. On the difficult subject of textual criticism, all the minister will need is found in Bruce M. Metzger's *The Text of the New Testament: Its Transmission, Corruption, and Restoration* (second edition), though J. Neville Birdsall in *The Cambridge History of the Bible*, ed. by Peter R. Ackroyd and Christopher F. Evans, Vol. 1, Ch. 11, is an excellent supplement; and Gordon D. Fee's chapter in *Biblical Criticism: Historical, Literary, and Textual*, by R. K. Harrison et al., redeems a book of otherwise doubtful worth.

Second only to the indispensable Greek New Testament is the need to have on hand a copy of the Old Testament in Greek, the Septuagint, often referred to by the symbol LXX. Childs's recommendation is for the older edition of Henry B. Swete, which is available only as a used copy and is fairly rare. The standard text is the Württembergische Bibelanstalt edition, edited by Alfred Rahlfs and published in Stuttgart, which is reasonably priced and will meet most pastors' needs. See the Bibliography for details of publication.

Greek grammars come in all shapes and sizes. There are the elementary textbooks, of which J. Gresham Machen is perhaps the best known in the United States, and H. P. V. Nunn, as revised by John Wenham, the most popular in

Great Britain. The more advanced include the work of A. T. Robertson, reprinted by Broadman Press, and the indispensable Blass-Debrunner-Funk, *A Greek Grammar of the New Testament and Other Early Christian Literature*. The four volumes of *A Grammar of New Testament Greek*, by J. H. Moulton, W. F. Howard, and Nigel Turner, are excellent as reference works and will illuminate many a preacher's texts. A grammar to read from cover to cover is Charles F. D. Moule's *An Idiom-Book of New Testament Greek* in its latest edition. This is not so daunting a task as may at first appear; but if the thought is enough to scare away those whose Greek has grown rusty, why not make a start with Nigel Turner's *Grammatical Insights Into the New Testament*, or the same author's marvelously suggestive *Christian Words*? I guarantee your interest will be amply rewarded as sermon suggestions leap from the page. Even simpler is Ronald A. Ward's *Hidden Meaning in the New Testament: New Light from the Old Greek*, also written with an eye on the preacher's need.

Lexical data are always an essential part of adequate sermon preparation as well as a good control on our exegetical flights of fancy. All we can desire is supplied by Bauer-Gingrich-Danker, *A Greek-English Lexicon of the New Testament and Other Early Christian Literature*. Danker's name is a sign of the second edition (1979), replacing Arndt's in the 1957 edition. The later edition is the one to possess. In default of the large Bauer volume, I have found much profit in G. Abbott-Smith's *A Manual Greek Lexicon of the New Testament*, a book on my shelves with its spine broken from constant use. That usually says something about a book's practical worth! Liddell-Scott-Jones, *A Greek-English Lexicon* (9th ed., 1940), is the standard work for classical studies, but pastors will be able to make do with the abbreviated edition, usually obtained secondhand, though it is apparently still in print.

Before we leave the subject of resources to assist our Greek knowledge, let me mention a few other books of great value. First, as an aid to serious Gospel study we all need a synopsis of the Gospels, and the prime choice is Kurt Aland's

Synopsis Quattuor Evangeliorum. (Despite its Latin title, the book is accessible to all who can use New Testament Greek. A Greek-English edition, entitled *Synopsis of the Four Gospels*, is published by the United Bible Societies.) There are various counterparts to this aid, which print the English text, notably B. H. Throckmorton, *Gospel Parallels*, and F. L. Cross's translation of the Huck-Lietzmann *Synopsis*, but these are really second best. An exception is the Huck-Greeven *Synopsis*, a first-class resource, published in 1981 and now available in the United States.

Reuben J. Swanson's *The Horizontal Line Synopsis of the Gospels* offers a conspectus of the English texts in vertical columns, with agreements underlined. A start has been made toward producing an equivalent in Greek with textual variants, and so far *Matthew* has appeared.

Concordances in Greek are mainly for the academician, with the standard Moulton and Geden now superseded by H. Bachmann and H. Slaby (eds.), *Computer-Konkordanz zum Novum Testamentum Graece* and the less complete but very useful *Statistik des neutestamentlichen Wortschatzes*, by Robert Morgenthaler. More immediately serviceable is Clinton Morrison's *An Analytical Concordance to the Revised Standard Version of the New Testament*, which provides excellent and comprehensive coverage, enough to satisfy most needs. Of the older works there is the ancient *Cruden's Concordance*, which has done yeoman service, though it is incomplete in parts and is based on the King James Version. Robert Young's *Analytical Concordance to the Bible*, or James Strong's *The Exhaustive Concordance of the Bible*, or both, should therefore be sought out and kept at one's elbow.

IV
English
Translations

The choice of a suitable English translation of the New Testament is obviously an idiosyncratic affair, and no final ruling is possible. All that can be attempted here is to set down the relative merits and demerits of translations currently available, without overlooking older translations that have stood the test of time, though they may have fallen out of vogue in today's highly competitive market. Also a pastor's interest will vary according to whether he or she wishes to use the translation in the study or the pulpit or the adult Bible class.

The *King James Version* (the *Authorized Version* of 1611) has carved a niche for itself that remains. Its literary qualities and evocative appeal are beyond dispute, and many congregations, it seems, still prefer to hear scripture lections from this traditional rendering (or from the slightly modernized edition titled *Holy Bible: The New King James Version*, published by Thomas Nelson & Sons in 1979 and 1982). In Britain there is currently quite an influential movement which aims to restore both the 1611 translation and Cranmer's Prayer Book to the offices of public worship: witness the strongly-worded tractate, by several distinguished men and women of letters as well as theologians, titled *Crisis for Cranmer and King James*, published in 1979. Interestingly, as Massey H. Shepherd, Jr., points out (*The Psalms in Christian Worship*, p. 84), it is "only in the last two decades that many pastors and priests adopted the reading of lessons from contemporary translations," before that using invariably the *King James Version* or the Coverdale version of the Psalter in public worship.

The British *Revised Version* of the New Testament appeared in 1881, and it was intended to be, as its name implies, a revision of the *Authorized Version*, not a new translation, "except when in the judgment of the most competent scholars such change is necessary." The main advance was, of course, in the field of textual criticism, where the influence of Westcott and Hort can be seen to be dominant. The result is that the RV excels in being a faithful rendition of the best Greek text then available, but its concern for accuracy and precision make it more of a scholar's translation than one of wider appeal. "It has often been called a schoolmasters' translation, and there is much truth in this," comments F. F. Bruce (*The English Bible*, p. 142). The RV failed to replace the AV/KJV in public worship and private devotion.

American scholars were brought into the *Revised Version* project and suggested various criticisms and alterations. These were low-key, however, and kept in reserve until the *American Standard Version* appeared in 1901. This latter, like the RV, remains the most literal translation available—a boon to students tracing their way through the Greek text, but of limited appeal otherwise. The copyright was taken over by the International Council of Religious Education, representing churches in the United States and Canada, whose committee resolved in the 1930s to revise the ASV. The result was the *Revised Standard Version* (RSV), of which the New Testament was first published in 1946.

The *Revised Standard Version* has had a universal appeal to scholars and laypeople on both sides of the Atlantic; it is not difficult to see why. T. W. Manson summed up its merits: "It is reliable and . . . it speaks directly to the man in the pew in language he can reasonably be expected to understand." After nearly forty years that sagacious judgment, I believe, still stands.

But there are other options. At the top of the list is the *New International Version*. The New Testament part of this translation appeared in 1973 and has been subsequently revised in some minor matters, mainly, it would appear, in the direction of removing slightly ambiguous expressions. I realized this when at a church service I read from Matt. 16:22: "Peter took him aside and began to rebuke him. 'Perish the thought, Lord!' he said." A percipient member of the congregation spotted the expression, noting that it is British, not American, and discovered that I had read from the 1973 edition. His edition (1978) smoothed out the difficulty: "Never, Lord!" A small point, perhaps, but one needs to be aware of the latest revisions. See too I Cor. 12:28, where the latest revision drops the tendentious adverb "finally."

On the whole, the NIV translators have done a creditable job, and their work reads smoothly; it merits its place on the study shelf. In certain ways the flow of its narrative sections is an improvement on the RSV, even if occasionally its translation falls into theological traps avoided by the RSV. For example, the NIV rendering of Rom. 3:25, "through faith in his blood," is hardly supported by any recent commentators. And no alternative marginal reading is given.

The New English Bible, whose New Testament was published in 1961, was conceived with a more ambitious aim. It is not a revision but a new type of translation, with all the fresh opportunities and fearful hazards attendant on such an enterprise. Preachers' opinions have been predictably mixed. Some welcome its contemporary style and its effort to make "holy Scripture" come alive by a resort to "timeless" English prose. Often it succeeds admirably, and as a way to get the thread of Paul's argument in books like Romans or Galatians, it is great stuff. On the negative side, some readers find it stilted (Acts 17:18: Paul is described as "a propagandist for foreign deities"); and just occasionally it borders on the ludicrous (I Cor. 5:9: "Have nothing to do with loose livers," a phrase that will suggest to some frivolous minds a partner to "floating kidneys"). But these are unfair examples, since the entire New Testament work is a monument to careful scholarship, textual study, and the skill of the communicator—even if the audience is more highbrow than proletarian.

A much simpler version of the New Testament is the *Good News Bible*, which reads smoothly but often at the cost of strict accuracy and "literal" translation. It offers what is called "dynamic equivalence" in the interest of making the text intelligible—and has proved its worth. Its value as a study book is strictly limited, however, and its place in the pulpit may be questioned. The *GNB* (or *Today's English Version*, according to an earlier nomenclature) sacrifices the sense of the "numinous" to instant intelligibility; and preachers should be wary of "taking a text" from this translation, which is often paraphrastic. An even worse offender is, of course, *The Living Bible*, for which it is hard to find a good word to say.

So many people have been helped by J. B. Phillips' translation that it has again to be remarked that this noble effort was never intended to be more than a paraphrase. Based on a scholarly approach to the text, to be sure, it endeavored to give the wider sense ("holy kiss" became "handshake all round" in I Peter 5:14, to give a trivial example).

Much more solid is James Moffatt's translation, now neglected, which from its publication in 1913 was handicapped by some unusual Scottish expressions (the land "manager" (NIV) or "steward" (NEB) became in Moffatt's rendering a "factor," Luke 16:1—a rare case of obscuring the text for most readers). Yet Moffatt's best efforts are often brilliant. Read him at I Corinthians 13 or Phil. 3:20 ("We are a colony of heaven") and I think you will agree. The counterpart to Moffatt is, for American readers, Edgar J. Goodspeed's *The New Testament: An American Translation* (1923), which has worn well, and deservedly so. Charles K. Williams' translation, *The New Testament in the Language of the People* came along in 1937. He strove to be exact in his rendering of Greek tenses and moods, but the result is somewhat self-defeating and flat. At times he is plain wrong (see F. F. Bruce, *The English Bible*, p. 180). But he seems to have set a trend in producing "expanded" versions, that is, translations enlarged with parenthetic clauses to bring out what the translator feels is the correct nuance (or nuances). Kenneth S. Wuest tried this method in his three-volume work (1956–1959), and F. F. Bruce has done it in a more accomplished way more recently in his *An Expanded Paraphrase of the Epistles of Paul*, now obtainable in a 1981 reprint that adds the RSV text in a parallel column for the sake of comparison. *The Amplified New Testament* (1958) showed how this method can be taken to extremes that border on the absurd; and the legacy was to be taken up later in *The Living Bible* (1971), though mercifully without the elaborate use of brackets and strings of synonyms bringing to mind a page of Roget's *Thesaurus*.

The Jerusalem Bible is a Roman Catholic version that broke new ground in several respects. Originally published in France as *La Bible de Jérusalem*, it was published in English in 1966 and claimed to be "*the* modern Bible for the modern reader seeking a greater understanding and appreciation of the scriptures in the language and imagery of today," irrespective of denominational affiliation. Doctrinal peculiarities, to be sure, are virtually nonexistent, and the ecumenical spirit of the enterprise is so well known that many Protestants use this version without demur. Poetic or lyrical passages are printed as such, as in the hymns of the Nativity in Luke and in the hymnic sections Phil. 2:6-11 and I Tim. 3:16. Each pericope has an appropriate descriptive heading, a feature that makes for easy reference and reading. The translation is well done and attractively presented, and the questionable decision to print the divine covenant name as Yahweh in the Old Testament did not apply to the New in its quotations from the Old, for which one is grateful.

V
Bible Dictionaries and Encyclopedias

For information on Bible dictionaries and encyclopedias, F. W. Danker's full chapter should be consulted, supplemented by the lengthy article by Wilbur M. Smith in the revised *International Standard Bible Encyclopedia (ISBE)*. The latter extends the list up to the English translation of the Kittel-Friedrich *Wörterbuch*, called *Theological Dictionary of the New Testament*, translated by Geoffrey W. Bromiley in nine volumes. Most readers will by now have reached a personal decision, whether influenced by James Barr or not, on the usefulness of "Kittel" in its English dress and in those imposingly stout volumes. The earlier volumes are naturally out of date on many counts as well as vulnerable to Barr's shafts of objection. The later volumes reflect a more thoroughgoing commitment to tradition-historical criticism and have more of a strictly exegetical component (see, e.g., Eduard Schweizer on "soma" [body] in Vol. 7). But Kittel still remains a first-rate resource dictionary of New Testament *theology*; as such it has both strengths and weaknesses.

The chief strength of Kittel can be measured against its nearest rival, *The New International Dictionary of New Testament Theology*, in three volumes. This is a translation of a German work titled *Theologisches Begriffslexikon zum Neuen Testament*, a mini-Kittel, but more conservatively inclined, expanded by a team of English-speaking scholars, mainly evangelical, under the leadership of Colin Brown. A notable feature is the very full bibliography in both English and the

Continental languages. There are also extensive discussions of key theological concepts, such as "resurrection" (fifty pages) and "word" (sixty-five pages). The value of *NIDNTT* for sermon construction is considerable, though it goes without saying (I hope) that the data have to be digested before we attempt to put this material into sermons.

The weakness of Kittel is obviously its incompleteness as a *Bible* dictionary. For a more extensive treatment we need a full-scale encyclopedia, and there are several multivolumed works in the bookstores. Probably the best is *The Interpreter's Dictionary of the Bible*, in four volumes, with a supplementary volume, published in 1976, that seeks to update the earlier (1962) publication but also adds fresh entries. This Abingdon set replaces the venerable Hastings' *Dictionary of the Bible*, in five volumes, which can still be profitably consulted. *The Zondervan Pictorial Encyclopedia of the Bible* is a poor substitute—though not lacking in intrinsic value—and is conservatively slanted. The *International Standard Bible Encyclopedia* (*ISBE*) has now reached two volumes in its revised form. It is marked by exhaustive (and sometimes exhausting) completeness. A more rigorous pruning of the old *ISBE* would have served modern readers better, in my judgment. Abingdon has announced a new *Dictionary of Bible and Religion*, forthcoming, which will, I estimate, be a potted edition of *The Interpreter's Dictionary of the Bible* and will serve the needs of the busy pastor and the lay Bible class teacher in an admirable manner and with broader scope than *IDB*.

One-volume dictionaries also cater to a wide spectrum of tastes and interests. The one with the widest appeal to evangelicals is *The New Bible Dictionary* (1982 edition), revised from its 1962 dress. This revision was also sumptuously illustrated and issued in three volumes under the title *The Illustrated Bible Dictionary* in 1980. It is quite an investment, though sometimes it is discounted in bookstores when the set is bought outright. The text (without illustrations) is available in one volume, but the color illustrations are so appealing and helpful that I recommend buying the three-volume work if at all possible. An alternative is *The New Westminster Dictionary of the Bible*, showing serious signs of its 1944 publication date, though it was revised in 1970, when "New" was added to its title. In 1963 Frederick C. Grant and Harold H. Rowley revised the one-volume edition of James Hastings' *Dictionary of the Bible*, but alas, this revision is now out-of-date.

If we move on to include Wordbooks under the rubric of New Testament Dictionaries, there are several titles that often escape notice, to the preacher's detriment. One is Alan Richardson's *A Theological Word Book of the Bible*, which holds many treasures. For instance, read Reginald H. Fuller on "Church, Assembly" or Christopher R. North on "Sacrifice" to see the great value of these and other entries.

The second book corresponds roughly to Richardson's in scope and stance: it is *The Vocabulary of the Bible* (also published as *Companion to the Bible*), edited by Jean-Jacques von Allmen. I have used this volume with great profit. I doubt if there is a more compact essay on "Marriage" anywhere than in Von Allmen's six pages under that heading; and the team effort of Edmond Jacob and H. Mehl-Koehnlein on "Man" produces a mini-theology of humankind in as many pages. Harold H. Rowley's commendation and hope that this book "will bring about a revival of theological preaching" accurately sums up the raison d'être of the entire work.

VI
New Testament
Introductions

Textbooks that are part and parcel of one's ministerial education in seminary or theological college tend to get the cold-shoulder treatment after graduation and ordination. This is a great pity, though the reaction is understandable enough.

Students who have worked their way through Werner G. Kümmel's *Introduction to the New Testament*, even in its more presentable second edition translated and edited by Howard Clark Kee, will recall their sense of relief upon learning that, for examination purposes, they never need open that volume again. Kümmel's text well illustrates the adage, *Le secret d'ennuyer est celui de tout dire.* But there is discipline involved in consulting Kümmel, even if he does try "to say everything." His *Introduction* therefore deserves a continuing place on our library shelf as a reference tool to be consulted from time to time.

Another mammoth one-volume *New Testament Introduction* (in its third edition) is Donald Guthrie's title. This steers a middle course on many issues, veering to a traditionalist view on disputed matters of authorship, dating, and place on the New Testament trajectory. It is certainly a compendious handbook, with a section on each Gospel and letter to describe the content. But the theological thrust is minimal, and little is acknowledged of the creative power of "situations" in the early church that most likely were the occasion of the various documents. Everett F. Harrison's *Introduction to the New Testament* is simpler, less full, but more attractively

presented and, with Robert H. Gundry's more recent *A
Survey of the New Testament*, admirably fills a needed spot as a
quick reference work. My own two-volume *New Testament
Foundations: A Guide for Christian Students* attempts to sketch
what materials students would need to set the New Testament books in their historical and cultural background, with
an emphasis also on the theological message. A different
theological emphasis is seen in Norman Perrin's *The New
Testament, An Introduction* (second edition, revised by Dennis
C. Duling). Having the same general interest is Eduard
Lohse's more popular *The Formation of the New Testament*, as
well as the somewhat dated Willi Marxsen, *Introduction to the
New Testament* (third edition), which has the happy knack of
saying a lot in a few words. Catholic scholarship is ably
represented by Alfred Wikenhauser's *New Testament Introduction*, which I have referred to frequently for its lucid
presentations.

Students in my generation were brought up on James
Moffatt's *An Introduction to the Literature of the New Testament*
(now more of a museum piece), and more profitably on Alan
H. McNeile's *An Introduction to the Study of the New Testament* (revised by C. S. C. Williams). The latter is a most
readable book, and I still recommend it—provided it is
supplemented by a book like Reginald H. Fuller's *A Critical
Introduction to the New Testament*, which is written with a light
touch but often sharply focused judgments. The oral presentation of Fuller's material in the classroom is preserved by the
layout of the book, and that feature is an asset.

Smaller books that essay the task of describing the contents
of the New Testament are legion. We mention only those
that have made their appeal: There is A. M. Hunter, particularly his insightful and seminal *The Unity of the New Testament*, which now needs to be counterbalanced by James
D. G. Dunn's *Unity and Diversity in the New Testament*. Also
there is Oscar Cullmann's simple guide to the New Testament literature, and, best of all, Brian E. Beck, *Reading the
New Testament Today*—an excellent model to follow, and full

of wisdom for the pastor as well as the student. Slightly fuller but altogether admirable as an introduction to New Testament criticism is Charles F. D. Moule, *The Birth of the New Testament*, especially in its third revised edition. I suspect that Moule's book will prove an eye-opener and a creative catalyst to ministers who left college or seminary more than twenty years ago, and I can foresee Moule's insights finding their way into a lot of sermons—to everyone's advantage.

The history of New Testament scholarship is amply covered in Werner G. Kümmel's *The New Testament: The History of the Investigation of Its Problems*, which is a mine of information on the question of where German New Testament scholarship came from, especially the influence of the Tübingen school. Less compendious, and full of human interest—a feature sorely lacking in Kümmel—is Stephen Neill's *The Interpretation of the New Testament 1861–1961*, which highlights British contributions but which needs a revision to bring it up to date over the past two decades. If these two books look threatening, I commend F. F. Bruce's lucid overview of "The History of New Testament Study" in *New Testament Interpretation*, edited by I. Howard Marshall. It is an amazingly comprehensive survey—from Marcion to Fuchs—on the often erratic but always fascinating course of New Testament research and speculation across the centuries. An acquaintance with this story will give us perspective and wisdom in discerning what today's leading scholars are saying.

VII
Biblical History
and Background

Apart from the reader's having control of details supplied in most good and recent Bible dictionaries and handbooks, there is value in possessing a set of volumes that give an overview of the history of New Testament times. Probably the most serviceable is F. F. Bruce, *New Testament History,* an excellent and reasonably priced coverage of political, social, and religious movements from the Babylonian exile to the mid-second century of our era. To take up special points of interest, especially on the religious and philosophical setting of the first-century world, Helmut Koester's *Introduction to the New Testament,* Volume 1, can be recommended for its authority and interesting treatment. I should still prefer to read the actual texts of the period, and for that reason C. K. Barrett, *The New Testament Background: Selected Documents,* is a virtually indispensable tool, along with a more recent title by David R. Cartlidge and David L. Dungan, *Documents for the Study of the Gospels: A Sourcebook for the Comparative Study of the Gospels.* It centers chiefly on form-critical parallels with the Gospel materials.

Floyd V. Filson's *A New Testament History* used to be a student's main standby but is now superseded by the titles given above. Leonhard Goppelt, *Apostolic and Post-Apostolic Times,* is concerned much more with the life and growth of the church, its inner structure and organization. Bo Reicke, *The New Testament Era,* is less full than Bruce or Koester, and lacks sparkle. Hans Conzelmann has written a somewhat partisan history of the church across the decades of the New Testament period and into the second century in his *History of Primitive Christianity.* Yet this smallish book has considerable attraction, since it leaves the reader in no doubt that the historical characters, especially Paul, were real people of flesh and blood, not cardboard figures of older church historians.

This brings us to Paul, the colossus who bestrides the scene of the apostolic church, insofar as our New Testament tells the story. Older lives of the apostle, e.g., that of Conybeare and Howson, performed a good service, but their day is over. Options of the present time range from the eminently readable biography *Saint Paul,* by classical historian Michael Grant, to the more theologically slanted treatment by Günther Bornkamm, titled simply *Paul.* Falling somewhere in the middle range is F. F. Bruce's *Paul: Apostle of the Heart Set Free* (British title: *Paul: Apostle of the Free Spirit*), a very serviceable historical study. Other titles on Paul are best considered under the heading of New Testament Theology, yet there are two older books that I have used constantly since I bought them thirty years ago. The first can now sometimes be picked up secondhand; the second is available in reprint. I refer to C. A. Anderson Scott, *St. Paul: The Man and the Teacher,* and James S. Stewart, *A Man in Christ.* Of similar scope but with varying emphases are Martin Dibelius' *Paul,* revised by Werner G. Kümmel, and Arthur D. Nock's compact, readable guide, *St. Paul.* C. A. Anderson Scott and James Stewart, in my judgment, take the palm, even if they occasionally skirt around the modern critical problems. They offer much to the would-be expositor anxious to introduce Paul's life and teachings to a Bible class or congregation, and their lasting value is that they make Paul come to life. That surely is the least we can ask of any book on Paul. Herman Ridderbos, *Paul: An Outline of His Theology,* is a heavyweight treatment, making few concessions to our concerns as preachers, but is one of the few treatments from the Reformed viewpoint.

By comparison, current offerings under the caption Lives of Jesus are not very inspiring. These spread themselves thinly across the theological landscape from a conservative recital of the biblical data in Donald Guthrie (*A Shorter Life of Christ*) and Everett F. Harrison (*A Short Life of Christ*) to the radical positions taken in Herbert Braun (*Jesus of Nazareth: The Man and His Time*) and—to a lesser degree—in the classic outline of Hans Conzelmann titled *Jesus,* which has been translated from his well-known essay in the encyclopedia *Die Religion in Geschichte und Gegenwart* and is highly recommended. Still to be valued is Günther Bornkamm, *Jesus of Nazareth,* but it is now over two decades old; and Eduard Schweizer's *Jesus* lacks anything distinctive to commend it.

One exception to this somewhat dismal picture is Ben F. Meyer's *The Aims of Jesus,* a book that has tremendous evocative power and challenges a lot of current assumptions. Another title not to be missed for its role in getting us to think afresh about familiar themes in Jesus' ministry is A. E. Harvey, *Jesus and the Constraints of History.* Either book would immeasurably enrich any pulpit ministry.

Ministers should own at least one reliable atlas of New Testament topography. I recommend Lucas H. Grollenberg, *Atlas of the Bible,* or, if this is too far beyond one's means, the same author's paperback *The Penguin Shorter Atlas of the Bible,* which is firstrate for both its reliable information and its photography. *The Westminster Historical Atlas to the Bible,* edited by George Ernest Wright and Floyd V. Filson, is an excellent alternative, with the *Macmillan Bible Atlas,* edited by Yohanan Aharoni and Michael Avi-Yonah, a runner-up.

Historical geography is best studied in company with the acknowledged expert, Yohanan Aharoni, in his *The Land of the Bible* (revised and enlarged edition), though this guidebook covers mainly, Old Testament sites and ways. It replaces George Adam Smith's classic *The Historical Geography of the Holy Land,* which, however, has been reprinted in recent years.

The incidents of Jesus' ministry are illumined by Clemens Kopp, *The Holy Places of the Gospels,* an erudite work. More deftly written and fascinating in its approach is the highly commended *Jerusalem as Jesus Knew It,* by John Wilkinson, whose firsthand acquaintance with the region gives his book special authority and appeal, second only to Jack Finegan's *The Archeology of the New Testament* and John Thompson's wider coverage.

Paul's career in the Syrian Levant and the Mediterranean lands can be more intelligibly appreciated if we know a little about life in these cities and locales. The standard reference is Henri Metzger, *St. Paul's Journeys in the Greek Orient,* but it is profitable to dip into the voluminous writings of older scholars such as G. A. Deissmann and Sir William M. Ramsay, who knew the Anatolian terrain (modern Turkey) as few did in the nineteenth century. Indeed, Deissmann's *Light from the Ancient East* (fourth edition) is dated, but it still makes arresting reading from the pen of a master in papyrology and Greco-Roman social studies.

Howard Clark Kee's small book *Christian Origins in Sociological Perspective,* on the sociology of the New Testament, will alert the reader to more recent trends and open the door to the more ambitious works such as Abraham J. Malherbe, *Social Aspects of Early Christianity;* Gerd Theissen, *Sociology of Early Palestinian Christianity* (British title: *The First Followers of Jesus*); also his *The Social Setting of Pauline Christianity: Essays on Corinth;* and Wayne A. Meeks, *The First Urban Christians: The Social World of the Apostle Paul.* Later writers in this area pay tribute to an older, groundbreaking monograph by Edwin A. Judge, *The Social Pattern of Christian Groups in the First Century,* which should be sought out by anyone wishing to enter this field of inquiry, with some later criticism by Ronald F. Hock, *The Social Context of Paul's Ministry.* But a prerequisite is certainly Martin Hengel's *Judaism and Hellenism: Studies in Their Encounter in Palestine During the Early Hellenistic Period,* which provides the necessary orientation before one gets (unthinkingly?) drawn into this latest interest in New Testament studies. Hengel's shorter work *Jews, Greeks and Barbarians* is an updated version of his magisterial work, but more difficult to read because of its compressed style and format.

VIII
New Testament
Theology

By common consent it is in New Testament theology that the scholar has most to contribute to the pastor and preacher. Unlike Childs's Chapter VIII, which extends over just one page, this chapter will be more far-reaching. Perhaps the reason is that the options stand thicker on the ground in the New Testament field than is the case with the Old Testament, and that they reflect more consciously the philosophical presuppositions of the various writers.

All theology-making on the modern scene must come to terms with the vast and enduring influence of Ferdinand Christian Baur, whose Lectures on New Testament Theology were published posthumously in 1864. The following century attests to the great effect of the Tübingen school, whose history can be read in either Peter C. Hodgson (who writes appreciatively) or Horton Harris (whose stance is negatively critical). The two books offer antithetical judgments, which proves my point that Baur's influence is a force to be reckoned with.

The results of Baur's contributions, which we may summarize as commitment to developmental evolution as the ruling principle of New Testament theology, the polemical character of the New Testament documents, each of which has its own *Tendenz*, or distinctive viewpoint, and the function of New Testament criticism as descriptive, not normative, came to full growth in his successors: David Friedrich Strauss, Wilhelm Wrede, and Rudolf Bultmann. The story is best read in Robert Morgan's *The Nature of New Testament Theology*, or Gerhard F. Hasel, *New Testament Theology: Basic Issues in the Current Debate*. I have tried to state the points under discussion as I see them in a modest essay in *The Expository Times* in 1980: "New Testament Theology: Impasse and Exit." In this essay I have also attempted to spell out some criteria for constructing a New Testament theology, standing on the shoulders of Adolf Schlatter and particularly Peter Stuhlmacher, whose conclusion I regard as fundamentally sound, innovative, and "preachable": "The formation of the New Testament tradition [will have] the proclamation of Jesus Christ as Messianic Reconciler [as] its genuinely theological and critical center" (from *Historical Criticism and Theological Interpretation of Scripture*, a wonderfully provocative little book). The application of this *norma normans* to Paul may be seen in my *Reconciliation: A Study of Paul's Theology*.

Having declared a personal interest in this area—and readers deserve to know what an evaluator's own ideas are—I can proceed to assess current titles in the field of New Testament theology.

Pride of place goes to Rudolf Bultmann's two-volume *Theology of the New Testament*, not because all his conclusions may be acceptable, nor indeed because this is a "right-headed" book, but simply in view of its intrinsic value, its monumental importance for later scholars and for the church, and its quality of "aliveness." Not every theology generates the enthusiasm for its subject that is found in Bultmann's most significant treatise. It is surprisingly fertile in ideas for the preacher, whether or not one is a follower of Bultmann. Those who are initially hostile to "Bultmannianism," if they can be persuaded to read his *Theology of the New Testament*, are, I suspect, in for a pleasant surprise. His brilliant descriptive work is unexceptionable; where he forces many of us to part company is the point at which he shows Baur's influence and refuses a normative quality to the New Testament. But he is certainly worth reading on his own terms, often called "existentialist."

Hans Conzelmann, *An Outline of the Theology of the New Testament*, stands in the Bultmannian tradition but is more consciously designed as a classroom text. It is therefore most easily comprehensible than Bultmann's magnum opus and can be read with interest, though caution is necessary. "It makes in general much of the Bultmannian theology more palatable, but it still has problems of its own" is Joseph A. Fitzmyer's accurate comment.

At the other end of the theological scale I would place Ethelbert Stauffer, *New Testament Theology*, an immensely learned tome, critical of seeking parallels in Greco-Roman mysticism or Gnosticism, yet enriched by classical allusions and background. It *appears* to be ponderous, yet I used it repeatedly in my days of pastoral service and found it strangely suggestive and helpful for a pulpit ministry. One has to tease its worth out of the text, but the effort is well worth making. I recommend you try.

In terms of more immediate practical value, Werner G. Kümmel arranges the New Testament material according to the chief witnesses: Jesus, Paul, John, with a brief consideration of the faith of the primitive community. Kümmel is strong on New Testament unity: all the witnesses give consentient testimony to God's eschatological salvation in Jesus Christ; and it stands squarely in the Lutheran tradition. The New Testament functions as gospel, urging us to Christ. Not so markedly "Continental," but in the same tradition of "salvation history," is George E. Ladd's comprehensive *A Theology of the New Testament*, designed as a seminary textbook but of value to the working minister in his or her later career. One apparent weakness in Ladd's treatment lies in his failure to exploit the gains of redaction criticism in Gospel Christology and of tradition history in the epistles. James D. G. Dunn's books *Jesus and the Spirit* and *Christology in the Making* are at the other extreme, and thus highly influential and provocative. Dunn's arrangement and discussion of the New Testament background data are invaluable contributions. Whether what he deduces from those data is correct is more to be questioned (e.g., a denial that Jesus' preexistence is taught in Paul). But he has captured the fervency and drive of the first Christians in a way that few authors do. Pastors will read Dunn to great advantage and their own inspiration.

Alan Richardson's *An Introduction to the Theology of the New Testament* stays within the *heilsgeschichtlich* frame of reference but is more topical in its format. This can be an advantage in providing a thematic discussion of any chosen topic for the minister's preparation, but it loses the sense of dynamic unfolding of the kerygma that is seen in Oscar Cullmann's *The Christology of the New Testament*; Joachim Jeremias' *New Testament Theology* (only Volume 1 is available, on the Gospels); and Leonhard Goppelt's *Theology of the New Testament*. Cullmann's books (especially his earlier *Christ and Time*) still retain considerable usefulness, offering an easily presentable scheme of New Testament thought. I hazard the guess that most congregations can "take" Cullmann as served to them in a series of sermons on "promise and fulfillment" or the ascending time line from creation to consummation, with the midpoint centered in the cross and Easter victory. C. K. Barrett's *From First Adam to Last* shows how this might be done sermonically, though it is a scholarly book.

Jeremias' volume (*New Testament Theology: The Proclamation of Jesus*) catches our interest in Jesus' language forms and the message of the gracious Father who in Jesus calls his children to an open table fellowship and the joy of forgiveness and acceptance in his family. No preacher can fail to see how relevant these emphases are. Jeremias' book *The Parables of Jesus* has surely fed its message into many a sermon. It delivers us from the allegorizing and moralizing of the parables, the twin bane of the pulpit when sermons on Jesus' parables are announced.

Goppelt's *Theology of the New Testament* is less easily assimilable, but it is full of good things on the meaning of the public ministry of Jesus. Goppelt can help to answer the pressing question still haunting the preacher in the 1980s:

How may we preach the gospel from the Gospels? Too long we have been threatened by R. W. Dale's facile dictum (in his book *The Atonement*) that, "while He came to preach the gospel, His chief object in coming was that there might be a gospel to preach."

The latest one-volume attempt to capture the theology of the New Testament is Donald Guthrie's *New Testament Theology*, which runs to nearly a thousand pages. It is a notable achievement by any standard, and the author's magnum opus, crowning a lifetime of study, research, and teaching. The strength of the book is its assembling of the data in magnificent completeness; the weakness lies in its neglect of key areas, chiefly the development of Christology across the New Testament period, and the social implications of the gospel. Also, it fails to ask what are the hidden agenda questions that prompted the writing of the New Testament in the first instance. The principle on which Hans-Georg Gadamer insists (in *Truth and Method*) remains to place a question mark over many of Guthrie's learned pages: Is not interpretation the attempt to hear again the questions that occasioned the answers provided by the text?

A question like this brings us inescapably face-to-face with New Testament hermeneutics. An excellent starter is Walter Wink, *The Bible in Human Transformation: Towards a New Paradigm for Biblical Study*. When we are alerted to the issues of interpreting the text so that we can move with integrity from study to pulpit (in simple terms, when we consider *how* we can get from there to here, from the ancient world to our life today), we can progress to a consideration of the "new hermeneutic." The bibliography for this is in Anthony C. Thiselton's *The Two Horizons*, and more briefly in his essays on "Semantics" and "The New Hermeneutic," which he contributed to a well-documented primer, *New Testament Interpretation*, edited by I. Howard Marshall. If Thiselton's large book seems threatening—and it does make demands on the reader—I warmly commend Perry B. Yoder, *Toward Understanding the Bible*, as an excellent starter and a book full of practical common sense about reading the New Testament intelligently. We owe it to ourselves—and to our people in the pews—at least to try to wrestle with these issues as a precondition to moving *From Text to Sermon.* The latter is the title of a book by Ernest Best that discusses the theory in a cautious way; it is a pity, however, that there is little by way of positive encouragement to strengthen the preacher's arm. Leander E. Keck, *The Bible in the Pulpit: The Renewal of Biblical Preaching*; D. Moody Smith, *Interpreting the Gospels for Preaching*; and Reginald H. Fuller, *The Use of the Bible in Preaching*, are all useful titles with suggestions on preaching the New Testament in today's world.

Since many of our sermons are devoted—in intention at least!—to expounding the "gospel according to Paul," a final word may be added on what is a virtual library in itself. Books on Paul's message come with every kind of approach and interest.

I still think Leander E. Keck, *Paul and His Letters*, is one of the finest titles in the bookstores today; its semipopular format and reasonable price should not be despised. It will tell us more of the essential Paul than many a tome. I would also include Joseph A. Fitzmyer, *Pauline Theology: A Brief Sketch*, in this category. The latter has come back into print, and it can be also consulted in the *Jerome Biblical Commentary*, where it forms one of the major introductory essays.

And there are plenty of larger erudite works, both ancient and modern. In the first category I place C. A. Anderson Scott's *Christianity According to St. Paul*, for easy reference, fine writing, and obvious commitment to his theme as my number-one choice. Long since out of print, it will have to be searched for in used book shops. E. W. Hunt, *Portrait of Paul*, is less recommendable, though it is more recent. It still wears an old-fashioned look.

Paul against his Jewish background can be profitably studied with W. D. Davies' *Paul and Rabbinic Judaism* as guide and mentor, even if E. P. Sanders, *Paul and Palestinian*

Judaism, has made the picture more complex. Paul the Hellene is best seen through an older work: W. L. Knox, *Paul and the Church of the Gentiles*, again a recherché volume to be watched for on secondhand book lists.

It is Paul the Christian, as missionary apostle and theological thinker and pastor, who still captivates preachers and audiences today. The centrality of Paul's "conversion" is explored with great verve in Seyoon Kim's *The Origin of Paul's Gospel*—a welcome contribution from the Third World, as Martin Hengel notes in his foreword. If apocalyptic is the key to Pauline theology, as J. Christiaan Beker (*Paul the Apostle*) insists, the burning issue is how to relate this "old world" concept to our present day. Beker's smaller book *Paul's Apocalyptic Gospel* points the way; but at least one reader doubts that this is the true or safe or even possible direction to go. An ever-present danger, it seems to me, is that the "theology of the cross" gets pushed off center in Beker's work, while I admire his learning and am sure many pastors have profited by it.

More determinative for Paul, and for preachers of the Pauline message, would be books that place the *centrum Paulinum* in the cross; and for this reminder I know of nothing finer than the older works of James Denney (e.g., *The Death of Christ*) or the more recent books of Leon Morris, *The Apostolic Preaching of the Cross* and *The Cross in the New Testament*; also Nils A. Dahl, *The Crucified Messiah*; and Hans-Ruedi Weber, *The Cross: Tradition and Interpretation*. The last-named book is fertile in many ways, and combines exact scholarship with a warm exegetical spirit that relates the biblical material to our appreciation of that event at Calvary as the "hiding-place of God's power and the inspiration of all Christian praise," in Denney's oft-quoted words.

IX
Series
of Commentaries

The books to be included in our discussion of commentary series fall into three unequal categories.

First, there is at least one series that aims to offer *A Digest of Reformed Comment*. It is the work of a single compiler, Geoffrey B. Wilson. He has undertaken the herculean labor of distilling the best of Puritan, Reformed, and modern comment on the Pauline letters in a most attractive fashion, since these quotations are interwoven with his own observations on the text of Paul's writings from a pastoral viewpoint. In a sense, he has done our homework for us by consulting Calvin, the Puritan divines, and the nineteenth-century orthodox, and reproducing their most memorable obiter dicta on Paul. The result is a laudable effort, with only Philippians and the pastoral epistles still to be added to this compilation of comment on the apostle's writings. The result is a set of paperbacks well worth securing and keeping on hand at the sermon desk.

Secondly, there are just a few endeavors on the part of individuals to write single-handedly a commentary on each of the twenty-seven New Testament books. The best known is that of William Barclay, whose *Daily Study Bible* is so familiar and universally praised that further commendation is superfluous. He is, in my opinion, more successful with the epistles and Revelation than with the Gospels, where the approach is decidedly old-fashioned and "liberal" in theology. Read Barclay on Jesus' miracles to get the point. But the *Daily Study*

Bible is an amazing achievement, and many pastors have been grateful for Barclay's help in time of need.

Another large effort is by William Hendriksen, who began well with a commentary on the book of Revelation (titled *More than Conquerors*) but unhappily seems to have been diverted in his works on *Matthew, Mark,* and some of the Pauline epistles (notably on *Philippians* and *Colossians*). None of the succeeding books—the series is not complete—has much value, I fear, and parts of the treatment, such as the resort to charts and diagrams, border on the grotesque.

Thirdly, on the more serious level, there are the many-authored series. The *International Critical Commentary (ICC)* stands at the head of this list, and outstanding older volumes will be noted as we turn to the individual New Testament books. In brief, the still premier volumes are J. H. Bernard on *John,* William Sanday and Arthur C. Headlam on *Romans,* Archibald Robertson and Alfred Plummer on *I Corinthians,* and R. H. Charles on *Revelation.* Plans have beeen made for rewriting the volumes in this valued series, and Charles E. B. Cranfield's commentary on *Romans* in two volumes has already appeared. The great drawback, however, is that the writers presuppose a substantial linguistic ability on the part of readers. Quotations in Greek and Latin are left untranslated, and the depth of the erudition is sometimes forbidding to the average pastor.

The *Hermeneia* series recognizes these realities, and offers just as much detail as *ICC,* but mercifully comes to the rescue of those without a classical education by offering standard translations, chiefly from the Loeb edition, of the Greek and Latin authors cited. A number of the *Hermeneia* titles are translated from German originals (Eduard Lohse on *Colossians-Philemon,* Rudolf Bultmann on *The Johannine Epistles*), but Fortress Press in announcing the full roster of contributors indicates that the balance of the New Testament commentaries will have Americans or domesticated Americans as authors. (The exception is Hans Conzelmann's *Acts,* translated from *Handbuch zum Neuen Testament.*)

The *Anchor Bible* (*AB*) series is still in progress. Its limiting feature is one of unevenness: Raymond E. Brown on *John* is excellent; but Bo Reicke on *The Epistles of James, Peter, and Jude* suffers under an unfortunate restriction; and the team effort of William F. Albright and C. S. Mann on *Matthew* is regrettably a lost opportunity. The lesson to be learned is the need to discriminate, and with Professor Childs I recommend that would-be purchasers get just the volumes that excel in any given series and resist the temptation to buy the entire series carte blanche, notwithstanding publishers' discounts.

I recognize that my role in the *Word Biblical Commentary* (*WBC*) editorship will make any comment on it here an unseasonable judgment. However, three volumes—*Colossians-Philemon* (O'Brien), *I-II Thessalonians* (Bruce), *Jude-II Peter* (Bauckham)—have so far appeared in the series, which offers a new translation from the Greek, an attractive format for easy consultation, and an international group of contributors, some of whom are veterans (F. F. Bruce) and some rising luminaries (James D. G. Dunn, David E. Aune, Peter T. O'Brien, to mention only representatives from three continents). A parallel series is *The New International Greek Testament Commentary* (*NIGTC*), edited by W. Ward Gasque and I. Howard Marshall, which offers a substantial exegetical treatment based on the Greek text and involves an up-to-date use of sources and bibliography. Three volumes—*Luke* (Marshall), *Galatians* (Bruce), and *James* (Davids)—have been released so far and are given due recognition in Chapter XI, below.

I share Childs's hesitation over the value of *The Interpreter's Bible* (*IB*) and would endorse his remarks and cautions. The aim of the series was innovative, but impracticable, and in the event it failed to achieve its declared goal of combining historical scholarship and homiletical guidance. Neither side of the contributors' team seems to have understood the opportunity for cross-fertilization; and the result is a rather nebulous product, which to call a hodgepodge would be uncharitable, but somewhere near the mark.

The *New International Commentary on the New Testament* (*NICNT*)—published in Britain as the *New London Commentary on the New Testament*—has also been a long time in reaching completion. The earlier volumes (J. Norval Geldenhuys on *Luke;* E. K. Simpson on *Ephesians*) are sorely in need of an overhaul. The later books are much more important, e.g., William L. Lane on *Mark* and Robert H. Mounce on *Revelation.* But here again the call is to pick and choose, and it would be disastrous to invest in the entire series for the sake of a few outstanding items. A notable series that will appeal to pastors who have difficulty with Greek is *Harper's New Testament Commentaries* (*HNTC*) (published in Britain as *Black's New Testament Commentaries*). This series is an Anglo-American venture by A. & C. Black and Harper & Row. The chief aim is lucid comment on the text, freshly translated but not requiring a knowledge of Greek for comprehension. There are already some distinguished titles in this series, notably C. K. Barrett's three volumes (on *Romans, I Corinthians, II Corinthians*) and George B. Caird on *Revelation.*

The *Harper-Black* series, at present under way and not yet complete, virtually replaces the old *Moffatt New Testament Commentary* (*MNTC*), which is becoming severely dated. Based on Moffatt's translation, it served a very useful purpose in pre-World War II days. Some volumes, such as C. H. Dodd on *Romans,* remain collector's items. Other contributions may still command respect, e.g., James Moffatt on *I Corinthians.*

The *Broadman Bible Commentary* is a compact series, written by Baptist authors and chiefly expository in slant and appeal.

The *Westminster* series has some illustrious names on its roster, but it is so dated that it now holds chiefly an antiquarian interest, with one or two notable exceptions.

On the smaller scale I recommend the *New Century Bible* (*NCB*). Here, personal considerations aside, I believe there is excellent value in David Hill on *Matthew,* Hugh Anderson on *Mark,* Barnabas Lindars on *John* (a marvel of compression),

F. F. Bruce on *I-II Corinthians,* and George R. Beasley-Murray on *Revelation.*

The *New Clarendon Bible* seems never to have got going. Based on the New English Bible translation, only a few volumes have seen the light of day. The older *Clarendon Bible* is now obsolete.

Less space is available in the *Torch, Tyndale,* and *Pelican* series, where the occasion demands pithy comment and apposite remarks. The stance is best seen in I. Howard Marshall on *Acts* (a revision of E. M. Blaiklock) and F. F. Bruce on *Romans,* in the *Tyndale* series; or in J. L. Houlden on *Paul's Letters from Prison* and J. P. M. Sweet on *Revelation,* in the *Pelican* series. The *Tyndale* series is currently undergoing revision and will be based on RSV or NIV in place of KJV/AV.

The new *Interpretation* commentary series being published by John Knox Press is too recent to elicit an opinion, but the first volumes augur well for what is to come. Lamar Williamson (on *Mark*) and Charles Cousar (on *Galatians*) have evidently understood the aim of this project, which is to present each biblical book for its most effective use in preaching and to provide help by showing how the text stands in a wider context. Scripture is seen in its theological significance for faith and life today. This is an ambitious goal. From the same publishing house we already have a junior version of how this laudable aim may be achieved in the *Knox Preaching Guides* series, of which six paperback volumes are already in print, covering selected New Testament books. Fortress Press offers a parallel in its *Proclamation Commentaries* series.

Foreign-language commentary series include two that are highly technical—Meyer's *Kritisch-exegetischer Kommentar* (*MeyerK*) and Lietzmann's *Handbuch zum Neuen Testament* (*HzNT*); the names are those of the first editors. One of the more popular commentary series is *Das Neue Testament Deutsch* (*NTD*), of which some volumes (e.g., Eduard Schweizer on the Synoptics) have been rendered into English. The latest series, *Evangelisch-katholischer Kommentar* (*EKK*), is a joint Roman Catholic-Lutheran project, and is designed for ecumenical circles in the European churches and their pastors. We will note outstanding volumes in the above series as we comment on the individual commentaries.

In French the premier place in the category of a commentary series for preachers' use is held by *Commentaire du Nouveau Testament* (*CNT*), which began in 1949. Only eight volumes have been published (most of them noted in Chapter XI, below), and in a few cases there has been a revised edition. This series is excellent in every way: in format, up-to-date discussions, incisive comment—in fact, all that the busy pastor needs, if he or she can handle the fairly simple French.

More complex is the *Etudes Bibliques* (*EB*) series. These are usually large-scale works, solid and detailed, and intended more for the scholar and researcher.

Occasional reference is made in the following pages to more technical commentaries in the main European languages, e.g., Herder's *Theologischer Kommentar zum Neuen Testament,* an erudite Roman Catholic series often with more than one volume for the biblical book discussed. The Protestant counterpart is *Theologischer-Handkommentar zum Neuen Testament,* equally learned, theologically angled, and mainly conservative in position. Both German series are incomplete.

Lastly, older series such as *The Expositor's Bible* and *The Expositor's Greek Testament* are referred to in just a few recommendations.

X
One-Volume
Commentaries

The chief merit of the one-volume commentary is its compactness and utility as a resource for those in a hurry. It also serves to provide a check on one's imagination, which can easily be fired by reading some more individualistic commentator or partisan source. Usually the one-volume works allow little scope for innovativeness; they report the current consensus of opinion. So we can quickly see what the middle-of-the-road scholars are saying. This is a useful feature, to save us from the more egregious mistakes we can unwittingly make in exegesis and sermon construction.

The commendation just given certainly applies to the outstanding title in this category: *The Jerome Biblical Commentary* (*JBC*), edited by Raymond E. Brown and others. This large handbook is valuable on several counts. It contains a succinct commentary on each biblical book, with pointed remarks and ample bibliography provided by leading Catholic scholars. Of equal value, moreover, are the essays interspersed in the text, which aim to bring the reader up to date on the latest results of biblical research. The essays justifiably claim to give "the state of the art" as it was perceived in 1968, when the *JBC* appeared. Naturally much water has flowed under several bridges since then, but, e.g., Raymond E. Brown's essay on "Hermeneutics" still is one of the best; and Joseph A. Fitzmyer's pages on "Pauline Theology" are a minor monograph, of first-rate service to all readers who wish to see quickly what are the issues at the cutting edge of Pauline research.

The Protestant counterpart—though one would never be able to tell the churchly allegiance of the contributors of this book or of *JBC*—is *Peake's Commentary on the Bible,* edited by Matthew Black and Harold H. Rowley. The commentary was written by our stellar authorities as they shone in the academic sky in 1962; happily, two decades later many of them are still there. Nonetheless *Peake* now stands in need of a revising hand, even if the exegesis provided is still very worthwhile. The articles that interlace the text are less full than those in *JBC* but are still first-rate. Witness George Ogg on "New Testament Chronology," an admirable conspectus by an expert, even if Robert Jewett and George B. Caird more lately have questioned some parts of its scheme. The strength of *Peake* (an entirely new work in 1962, but retaining the name of Arthur S. Peake, editor of the original *Peake's Commentary,* out of respect) lies in its exegesis, and every student and preacher will be glad to turn to it on occasion.

Not as extensive or as ecumenical in scope and stance is *The New Bible Commentary Revised,* edited by Donald Guthrie and others. A confessedly evangelical publication, this work is more flexible than its predecessor, at least on its exegetical pages. The treatment is purposely kept "simple," with barely a glance at critical issues. But its strength for many readers will be precisely in its straightforward exposition of what the Bible text teaches. A few contributors have expressed in nontechnical language the results of their more detailed studies appearing in other places: I. Howard Marshall on "Luke" and George Beasley-Murray on "Revelation" are clear examples.

Even more simple are the *Wycliffe Bible Commentary,* which is a nondescript work, and *The New Layman's Bible Commentary in One Volume,* the product of Christian Brethren authors, and edited by G. C. D. Howley and others (British title: *Bible Commentary for Today*). The New Testament part of the latter work, published separately as *A New Testament*

Commentary, represents some notable contributions along with more pedestrian writing. But these volumes need to be supplemented by our consulting the larger, more transconfessional works mentioned earlier. Breadth of treatment is highly desirable if we are to expose ourselves to new truths and fresh insights, and if we are to see the biblical texts through other eyes. Granted, we may come back to our confessional position as the place where we find our preaching convictions best expressed, but we shall hold our cherished beliefs with more confidence and greater wisdom (and, it is hoped, increased charitableness) if we have seen what other Christians understand as their exegetical findings.

XI
Individual
Commentaries

This will obviously be the lengthiest chapter as we survey what are, in one person's judgment, the best titles to look for in the field of commentary writing on a book-by-book basis. There are two overriding considerations, namely (*a*) what are the books of a former generation that have had an enduring influence and are accessible in larger library collections or purchasable, from time to time, in used book shops; and (*b*) what books are available in the current marketplace and worth acquiring. The interests of pastors, preachers, and teachers have been kept uppermost, with an occasional glance in the direction of the scholar and the research student.

Students at the beginning of their academic and ministerial career often ask that someone provide them with a clear-cut recommendation of a single title as the "best buy," similar to the way reviewers of gramophone records mark a special recording as "outstanding." I have responded to this desire at the end of each section. Sometimes two or more commentaries are tied for first place, and I have so indicated.

1. MATTHEW

After several decades of dearth when it was difficult to recommend a good full-scale commentary on Matthew's Gospel (in English, at least), we are faced with a number of choices. Robert H. Gundry's *Matthew: A Commentary on His Literary and Theological Art,* incorporating the techniques of midrashic comparison and redaction criticism, vies with Francis W. Beare's more traditionally conceived commentary. Beare's volume carries the lighter touch and is easier to use as a tool, but some of his historical judgments will provoke disagreement. Gundry's book also has raised a debate and will be valued more for its interest in Matthew's purpose than as an aid to preachers. David Hill's slightly older and more compact study (*NCB*) is a commentary in the traditional sense and full of exegetical insight; it stands out as serviceable and less expensive. If Hill's book is used alongside some monographs on Matthew's role as theologian and church teacher (a term made familiar by Krister Stendahl's *The School of St. Matthew*, 1954), the combination will be all the preacher needs.

Among monographs on Matthew's role as theologian and church teacher I would place *Tradition and Interpretation in Matthew*, by Günther Bornkamm, Gerhard Barth, and Heinz J. Held; this volume is a basic tool to show the gains of redaction criticism for the preacher. Another useful volume is *The Setting of the Sermon on the Mount*, by W. D. Davies, which needs to be complemented now by Robert A. Guelich's excellent recent study *The Sermon on the Mount*, on Matthew 5–7. And see also *The Theme of Jewish Persecution of Christians in the Gospel According to St. Matthew*, by Douglas R. A. Hare. Last (but not least by any means) is a most helpful exposition of recent work on Matthew's Christology by Jack D. Kingsbury titled *Matthew: Structure, Christology, Kingdom*. This brings up to date the information in Edward P. Blair's fine *Jesus in the Gospel of Matthew*, which unfortunately never found a British publisher.

An older work (on the Greek text) by A. H. McNeile still has value but is severely dated. For a penetrating study of Matthew's Gospel pericope by pericope, there is still nothing to rival Pierre Bonnard in the French *CNT* series, which ought to have been translated into English. William F. Albright and C. S. Mann (*AB*) join to produce a serviceable, if not too exciting, effort, with a good introduction to the

Gospel. There are helpful exegetical aids in Floyd V. Filson
(*Harper-Black*), J. C. Fenton (*Pelican*), and J. P. Meier. Eduard
Schweizer's succinct commentary is a translation of his contribution to *Das Neue Testament Deutsch* (*NTD*), and when used
in conjunction with Hill will be found to complement that
volume nicely. Both books fulfill the promise of the series of
which they form a part: they are basically exegetical tools,
which every preacher will need to keep within arm's length in
the study.

Preachers who turn to Matthew's Gospel for a text will be
less concerned with studies about Matthew's literary usage
(seen in M. D. Goulder's pioneering work and now in
Gundry's book, mentioned above) than with the evangelist's
role as church leader and teacher. Here redaction criticism
can be of real assistance, as noted above, but T. W. Manson's
The Sayings of Jesus should not be ignored, since it provides a
virtual commentary on Jesus' teaching in this Gospel as
understood in the pre-Bornkamm era.

RECOMMENDATION: Either Hill or Schweizer.

2. MARK

In my volume on *Mark* in the *Knox Preaching Guides* series,
edited by John H. Hayes, there is a list of commentaries I
found most serviceable in preparing that booklet. High on
the list are Hugh Anderson's work in *NCB* and William L.
Lane in *NICNT*. Both are clear, level-headed, and up-to-date
expositions of Mark's message as gospel with emphasis on the
historical and theological interest. For more detailed study
based on the Greek text, Charles E. B. Cranfield and Vincent
Taylor may be recommended, with the former more adapted
to easy reference. Both books are becoming dated, however,
since both were written before the gains of redaction criticism
could be utilized. For the ground-breaking redactional study,
Willi Marxsen's *Mark the Evangelist* should be consulted.

In commentary series proper, Sherman E. Johnson
(*Harper-Black*), A. E. J. Rawlinson (*Westminster*), and Dennis

E. Nineham (*Pelican*) contain nothing that cannot be found in the books mentioned above, but of these three, Nineham has the acutest theological sense, and he writes in a limpid prose style—a trait not all commentators share! Eduard Schweizer's work translated from *Das Neue Testament Deutsch* (*NTD*) is full of insights and application, and it should be within the preacher's reach. I personally found Josef Schmid's volume from the Catholic *Regensburg New Testament* series, translated and published in Cork, Ireland, a most helpful treatment, and full of good things. It is the only volume in this German Catholic series available in English, and it would be a pity if we were denied more of the excellence of this sample.

Of slender dimension but useful for quick reference is Paul J. Achtemeier's volume in the *Proclamation Commentaries* series. Etienne Trocmé's *The Formation of the Gospel According to Mark* is written with Gallic verve and offers a novel view of the Gospel. For example, his treatment of Mark's purpose in a missionary context is bound to spark several sermons.

For a series of sermons on Mark as passion story there is the collection of essays *The Passion in Mark,* edited by Werner H. Kelber. However, preachers will probably get more immediate value from Arland J. Hultgren's *Jesus and His Adversaries.* Mark 13 poses its own problems, and George R. Beasley-Murray's *A Commentary on Mark Thirteen* has not yet been superseded, though there have been later erudite volumes on that chapter, mainly in German. Finally, there is my own *Mark: Evangelist and Theologian,* an attempt to survey recent study of Mark. The ongoing sequel of Markan research from 1972 to 1979 may be read in Sean P. Kealy's valuable and unusual book *Mark's Gospel: A History of Its Interpretation,* which offers synopses of leading writers in the field and their works, arranged chronologically from the patristic period to our own day. See too James M. Robinson's updated *The Problem of History in Mark.*

RECOMMENDATION: Anderson stands first for its overall usefulness, but Lane is a close rival.

3. LUKE

There has been a flurry of scholarly activity centered on the Lukan writings since the 1950s, when W. C. van Unnik labeled Luke-Acts a "storm center of New Testament criticism." While much of this research and publication has been highly technical—and we may instance the debate focused on Hans Conzelmann's seminal *The Theology of St. Luke* (its original title, in German, was "The Middle of Time")—it should be recorded that the practical gains have been considerable and preaching resources have been enriched thereby. A good example is seen in Eduard Schweizer's popular lectures *Luke: A Challenge to Present Theology,* written as a parergon to his commentary on Luke in *NTD,* which is shortly to appear in the John Knox series of Schweizer's translated commentaries and will service the preacher's needs in the English-speaking world as *NTD* does on the European scene.

More erudite, yet eminently worth reading as sermon preparation, are Joseph A. Fitzmyer's *Anchor Bible* commentary (at present covering Luke 1–9), and I. Howard Marshall in *NIGTC.* The former is less demanding on the Greekless reader, and less taxing on the eyesight, than Marshall's closely packed pages, which in format are slightly self-defeating. A more thoughtful editorial pen would have helped in the earlier stages of this work, but there is no denying the mass of excellent material now available to aid the preacher and teacher who tries to understand Luke's Gospel.

Students of Greek will still need to refer to J. M. Creed (*Macmillan*) as to Alfred Plummer (*ICC*), both of which are dated in a double sense. They show their age as books written several decades ago, and they inevitably predate Conzelmann and the concerns raised specifically over Luke's work as an editor with a theological bent to his purpose. For orientation here we commend I. Howard Marshall's *Luke: Historian and Theologian,* as well as the essays in *Interpreting the Gospels,* edited by James Luther Mays, a most useful book for getting abreast of current study on all four Gospels, and one written with preachers and teachers in mind.

Serviceable commentaries, with much to offer in the field of exegesis, are those by A. Robert C. Leaney (*Harper-Black*) and E. Earle Ellis (*NCB*). In shorter compass are George B. Caird (*Pelican*) and Leon Morris (*Tyndale*). William Manson (*Moffatt*) is a slight disappointment to those who were helped by his insightful *Jesus the Messiah;* and J. Norval Geldenhuys (*NICNT*) could safely be passed over, except that his warm, devotional spirit exudes on every page, and this book will warm the heart if it fails to excite the imagination or stimulate the mind.

Mind-stretching can be left to the European interpreters of Luke; witness the collected essays in *Studies in Luke-Acts,* edited by Leander E. Keck and J. Louis Martyn, and more recently the survey of Robert Maddox, *The Purpose of Luke-Acts,* written at Munich and giving a richly comprehensive overview of all possible options currently expressed by German, French, British, and American scholars.

For detailed analytical treatment there is nothing to rival Heinz Schürmann's edition (as far as ch. 9) in the first volume in the *Herder* series. Smaller in size, but with theological sensitivity, is Walter Grundmann's work in the series aptly named *Theologischer Handkommentar.*

I personally found Bo Reicke's little book *The Gospel of Luke* rewarding. Though not a commentary in the strict sense, it held out several insights as sermon starters. And the same verdict holds for Helmut Flender, *St. Luke: Theologian of Redemptive History,* which, though not easy to read, is also rewarding. This brings us to a consideration of special studies on Luke's Gospel.

Raymond E. Brown's *The Birth of the Messiah* is virtually required reading in the pastor's study at the Advent season. Both Matthew's Nativity stories and Luke's early chapters are examined in close detail. J. Gresham Machen's *The Virgin Birth of Christ* is a useful polemical treatise in defense of the dogma, but exegetically not very profitable. John McHugh, in *The Mother of Jesus in the New Testament,* has a lot of suggestive—some might say speculative—material on Luke's infancy narratives, but I discovered a lot of preaching material here, to my pleasant surprise.

Three titles ought to be read for our overall education on current Lukan studies, since all of these books are written in such a polished and attractive way that they do no disservice to "the most beautiful book there is" (as Renan called Luke's Gospel). They are: John Drury, *Tradition and Design in Luke's Gospel;* Eric Franklin, *Christ the Lord: A Study in the Purpose and Theology of Luke-Acts;* and C. K. Barrett, *Luke the Historian in Recent Study.* We owe it to our pulpit ministry to make the acquaintance of these authors who are, each in his own way, able to write *con amore* about Luke and his works.

Luke's Gospel seems to me to stand high on many a preacher's list of favorite New Testament books as offering a rich and fertile seedplot for sermons. Time spent wrestling with Luke's purpose and his role as pastor-evangelist, in addition to his role as the author of a second volume in the New Testament library, is a wise investment (see also the section on the Acts of the Apostles).

RECOMMENDATION: Marshall (*NIGTC*) has the most to offer as a resource book, but it will be overtaken by the more readable Fitzmyer when the latter's addition to *AB* is complete.

4. JOHN

John's Gospel is by common consent a treasure trove for preachers and teachers of the word. Yet it poses a set of problems that every generation must seemingly wrestle with on its own. In particular, the issues of historical value and the meaning of John's symbolism are the two interlocking questions that honest preachers must look squarely in the eye before they announce a text from the Fourth Gospel. Books that elucidate John's background and thought world are good;

but even better are the commentaries that help us unpack
John's message as part of the diversity of New Testament
truth. And that means the best commentators will be those
who write with a concern to explore John's theological
dimension at some depth, to do for our day what William
Temple's two volumes (*Readings in St. John's Gospel*) did for
his time. One representative example of this in-depth exegesis is Robert H. Lightfoot's commentary volume *St. John's
Gospel;* and from the Barthian standpoint Edwyn C. Hoskyns
and Francis Noel Davey have put together a stimulating—if
sometimes wayward—book, exegetically weak, but facing the
theological questions head-on.

For thorough exegesis there is no substitute for C. K.
Barrett on the Greek text. His volume should be our first
resource, as we are able to use it, before we move on. Rudolf
Schnackenburg's contribution to the *Herder* commentary series has now been translated in three volumes, which are
repositories of learning and information. A close partner to
these leaders in the field is Raymond E. Brown (two volumes
in *AB*), easier to use because there is no Greek language
barrier, and full of exegetical perception.

Rudolf Bultmann's massive work contains much data as
background material, but he is so erudite as to leave the
reader who has concerns other than discovering religious-
historical parallels rather breathless.

Both literary analysis and historical learning are worn
lightly by Barnabas Lindars (*NCB*), whose fat volume in a
series otherwise lean and sleek should be within arm's reach.
Another large volume, this one in the *NICNT,* is contributed by Leon Morris, replacing an unsatisfactory title in the
same series by Merrill C. Tenney. To a lesser extent R. H.
Strachan, John Marsh (*Pelican*), R. V. G. Tasker (*Tyndale*),
and Joseph N. Sanders (*Harper-Black*) have their place, and
occasionally offer insights. Among older works, that of F.
Godet (three volumes) has a rich vein of spiritual worth, with
practical applications. B. F. Westcott's two titles (one based

on the Greek and one on the English text) can be relied on for sober and scholarly, if not overly stimulating, research.

For genuine excitement in Johannine studies we need to turn to individual contributions that are not commentaries in the proper sense, except that the first named in our roster does offer a commentary-like approach throughout his book. I refer to C. H. Dodd's later work *Historical Tradition in the Fourth Gospel*. This book admirably supplements—as it completes—his earlier and pioneering study *The Interpretation of the Fourth Gospel*. Both books by Dodd are milestone works, and they cannot be neglected.

Modern individual monographs are virtually legion, and we mention only some representative samples. J. Louis Martyn's *History and Theology in the Fourth Gospel* broke new ground when it first appeared, and it has now been revised. Robert T. Fortna's literary criticism has some positive things to offer the exegete; it is titled *The Gospel of Signs*. The more recent studies of R. Alan Culpepper, *The Johannine School* (on the Johannine community of faith), and John Painter, *John: Witness and Theologian* (on the teaching of John concerning the Christian life), are both important. There is a lot of valuable discussion of past and recent research in Johannine studies in Stephen S. Smalley's *John: Evangelist and Interpreter*. A. M. Hunter's *According to John* is a popular survey of recent trends, useful for catching up on what the scholars are saying, though Robert A. Kysar's book *The Fourth Evangelist and His Gospel* is more comprehensive, if less readable.

RECOMMENDATION: The choice turns firmly on whether the Greek text presents a problem. If it does, Brown is preferable; but if not, Barrett stands out, especially in its second edition.

5. THE ACTS OF THE APOSTLES

For users of the Greek New Testament—or for those who wish to brush up on their Greek—F. F. Bruce's first commentary (in chronological order) on Acts may be recommended as

a good exercise in linguistic study. His second volume (in
NICNT) virtually made the contents of his first book available to a wider public, but still lacked—on his own admission—much of a theological dimension.

For that we turn to Ernst Haenchen's massive work,
translated from his *MeyerK* contribution, and surprisingly for
so technical a work of scholarship, it is rich in preaching
suggestions that alert readers will not be slow to appropriate.
For a succinct overview of theological issues in the study of
Acts, note Robert J. Karris, *What Are They Saying About Luke
and Acts? A Theology of the Faithful God.*

On the historical side, there is nothing to supersede the
five volumes of *The Beginnings of Christianity,* edited by F. J.
Foakes-Jackson and Kirsopp Lake, happily available in a
Baker reprint at a bargain price. Volume 4 is commentary,
and with some excellent exegetical notes it is still valuable.
All later commentators pay tribute to Kirsopp Lake, Henry J.
Cadbury (whose contributions to the five-volume work are of
first importance), and F. J. Foakes-Jackson as a trio whose
work has stimulated their labors. A. N. Sherwin-White, *Roman Society and Roman Law in the New Testament,* brings the
story up to date on the side of the early church's setting in the
Roman world.

What subsequent commentators have done with the mass
of scholarly data is, of course, an individual matter. Richard
P. C. Hanson (*New Clarendon*) and William Neil (*NCB*)
represent the best in sober, dependable, British scholarship,
but with little flair. C. S. C. Williams (*Harper-Black*) has a
more attractive presentation, and this may be classed as the
preacher's best standby. The older book of R. B. Rackham
(*Westminster*) is written from the "high" Episcopalian viewpoint but will greatly help the preacher, as will Everett F.
Harrison's volume and that of I. Howard Marshall (*Tyndale*),
who exegetes Acts within an evangelical context, but with a
sharp eye for theological motifs.

I have been helped by a lesser-known title, the commentary by J. Alexander Findlay. Now dated in many respects (it

appeared in 1934; second edition 1936), it still gets to the
heart of the story of the early church, and in pericope after
pericope the writer's ability to expound the meaning of the
text in a set of broad strokes makes this work remarkably
fresh and relevant today. In fact, hard-pressed preachers
needing exegetical help fast are recommended to seek out
this title (available only in libraries and possibly in used book
stores) and use it alongside Gerhard Krodel's equally attractive and up-to-date contribution to the *Proclamation Commentaries* series, valuable for its literary analysis of Acts.

Not much good is done by Johannes Munck's *Anchor Bible*
volume, sad to say. There is some compensation, however, in
what is offered by a fellow Scandinavian, Jacob Jervell, in
Luke and the People of God: A New Look at Luke-Acts, even if
this book promotes a thesis (Luke's purpose is governed by
Jewish connections and his desire to keep the church and the
synagogue together) that lacks cogency. Robert Maddox's
The Purpose of Luke-Acts, mentioned earlier, should be consulted to get one's bearings on current options for interpreting the purpose of Acts. And no understanding of where
scholars are today is really possible without a knowledge of
where they have come from. For that reason W. Ward
Gasque's *A History of the Criticism of the Acts of the Apostles*
fills an important gap.

Studies on special themes in Acts are legion; and we may
content ourselves with mentioning only a few, selected by the
criterion that they are related to pastoral problems: Schuyler
Brown, *Apostasy and Perseverance in the Theology of Luke;*
James D. G. Dunn, *Baptism in the Holy Spirit* (first-class for
an exegetical treatment of problem passages such as Acts 8
and 19); Martin Hengel, *Acts and the History of Earliest
Christianity* (a robust essay in apologetics defending Luke's
role as an ancient historian); John C. O'Neill, *The Theology of
Acts in Its Historical Setting* (on Luke as an evangelist par
excellence); and Stephen G. Wilson, *The Gentiles and the
Gentile Mission in Luke-Acts* (valuable for some thoughts on
the church's mission in every age).

RECOMMENDATION: As a commentary to set one thinking, Haenchen is unrivalled; a different historical perspective will be found in Williams.

6. ROMANS

Commentaries on the pivotal epistle to the Romans as a key to Paul's theology and indeed to the New Testament teaching on salvation and salvation history come in all shapes and sizes.

Pride of place must go to Charles E. B. Cranfield's two-volume contribution to the revised *ICC*, though the older *ICC* by William Sanday and Arthur C. Headlam should in no way be disregarded. Their commentary is easier to use, and with less detail it will not tax the reader's patience and concentration; both virtues are needed to get the best out of Cranfield, who packs an amazing amount of detail into his exegesis. Every conceivable option is given, so that the reader knows what are the possibilities, both in the ancient church and among modern interpreters, before he learns how Cranfield inclines. In that sense Cranfield's *Romans* is a definitive work, and its objectivity is one of its foremost and finest assets. A close second is Ernst Käsemann's newly translated work, full of theological perception and marked by Teutonic *Gründlichkeit*. Fresh surprises await the reader at every turn, and one comes away from Käsemann with appreciation for Paul as a theologian, whether we agree with every position and argument of the commentator or not.

For practical purposes Franz J. Leenhardt's translated commentary has much to offer and is worth consulting. C. K. Barrett (*Harper-Black*) has put preachers in his debt with a plainly written but remarkably interesting commentary that goes to the heart of the Pauline gospel. For any preacher still unsure what that gospel was (and is), let me urge an acquaintance with Barrett's compact *Reading Through Romans* as a minor masterpiece, second to which is John A. T. Robinson,

Wrestling with Romans, which unhappily seems to run out of steam after treating ch. 8.

Commentaries that pursue a particular tack, that have what is called today a distinctive *Tendenz,* would include the dated work of C. H. Dodd *(Moffatt),* which represents the best in the older liberal tradition (see Dodd on the "wrath of God" in Romans 1, and his dismissive attitude to Romans 9–11); and John Murray *(NICNT,* 2 vols.), who views Romans through the spectacles of classical Reformed theology, much in the wake of Charles Hodge's mid-nineteenth-century commentary, reprinted in 1951. Of course, you may say that the latter is no bad thing, but prospective readers ought to be aware of a commentator's penchant.

In the field of smaller works, F. F. Bruce writes the *Tyndale* commentary with never a wasted word, and Handley C. G. Moule has given us two efforts in expounding the text of the epistle: a treatment of the Greek text *(Cambridge Bible for Schools and Colleges)* that is excellent, and a more devotional exposition in *The Expositor's Bible.* Brief comments on the text are found in A. M. Hunter's *Torch* edition and Ernest F. Scott's commentary. Special mention ought to be made of Matthew Black in *NCB* for two striking features: pointed comments on the text, and a remarkably full bibliography of recent work on Romans (up to 1973).

Karl Barth's *The Epistle to the Romans* (1922 ed.) is of course a classic. This book is the one that dropped like a bomb in the theologians' playground; but his *A Shorter Commentary on Romans* (1919) is very serviceable for getting to the nub of Barthian exegesis. From a strictly theological stance nothing is better than Anders Nygren's commentary, even if it fails as a verse-by-verse exposition. In the same tradition of Lutheran scholarship is the more succinct treatment by Roy A. Harrisville.

There are still other more devotionally and homiletically oriented books on Romans; we will mention John R. W. Stott's *Men Made New* (on Romans 5–8) and Earl F. Palmer's *Salvation by Surprise* (with useful study questions appended).

To shed light on a dark place (Romans 9–11) there is nothing more illuminating than *Christ and Israel* by Johannes Munck.

The list of foreign-language commentaries is headed by Otto Michel (*MeyerK* series) and Hans Lietzmann (*HzNT*), the former exegeting the text with great thoroughness, the latter offering pithy comments. A volume with more detailed scope and theological penetration is Ulrich Wilckens in the *EKK* series, designed with European clergy, both Catholic and Protestant, in mind.

RECOMMENDATION: Cranfield is a clear leader for sound and sober exegesis, but you cannot go wrong with Barrett (*Harper-Black*). The two titles complement each other and often disagree on points of detail.

7. I CORINTHIANS

C. K. Barrett (*Harper-Black*) has written the model commentary on I Corinthians, one that is not likely to be superseded in our generation. It is renowned for its lucidity as well as its comprehensiveness, with theological exegesis its forte. There are some shorter works that offer insights within a limitation of space: F. F. Bruce (*NCB*) and Jean Héring (translated from *CNT*) head the list.

For rigor and penetration there is nothing to touch Hans Conzelmann's commentary in the *Hermeneia* series. Its amazingly full treatment and bibliographical control make it indispensable for serious study. It will require some acquaintance with the Greek text, but not menacingly so, since translations are usually provided. To sharpen our Greek skills we have found R. St. John Parry's volume in the *Cambridge Greek Testament* (which has been on our shelves since student days, when it was the prescribed college text) very suggestive—though its point of view is now dated and reflects a period before "Gnosticism in Corinth" (Walter Schmithals' title) made its impact on commentators wrestling with the nature of the Corinthian problems. Nonetheless this handy commentary is full of exegetical insights, which do not go out of fashion.

The setting of I Corinthians in the Hellenistic milieu of a Greek city such as Corinth is accurately depicted by James Moffatt in the *Moffatt* series, while classical parallels and much erudition are featured in Archibald Robertson and Alfred Plummer's joint venture for *ICC*. The latter is still a book to be reckoned with. The social setting of I Corinthians has been discussed in many recent studies, the most noteworthy of which is Gerd Theissen's newly translated *The Social Setting of Pauline Christianity*.

In a smaller format there is a cluster of useful books as propaedeutic. First in order of preference is Margaret E. Thrall's excellent volume in the *Cambridge Bible Commentary* series. Her pithy comments go directly to the heart of the matter and are, again and again, on target as exegetical contributions. Next is Leon Morris' volume in the *Tyndale* series, which is marked by apposite comments and applications that alert preachers can utilize with ease and facility. Then comes John Ruef's volume in the *Pelican* series, again a small book packed with good ideas, as is Jerome Murphy-O'Connor's tightly written exposition. For something even more directly transferable from the study to the pulpit there is that exceptional treatment of William Baird titled *The Corinthian Church: A Biblical Approach to Urban Culture.* This is a fine blend of scholarship and pastoralia, and can be warmly commended.

Older volumes (e.g., Charles Hodge) and larger books (e.g., F. W. Grosheide in *NICNT*) may be kept in reserve, but their value is severely limited. F. Godet (in two volumes) and Marcus Dods (*Expositor's Bible*) have been preachers' standbys in the past, but alas, a new generation of commentators tends to supersede these former masters.

Hans Lietzmann's volume (*HzNT*), revised by Werner G. Kümmel, represents a resourceful treatment in German, though most of its usefulness is subsumed under Conzelmann's magisterial work in English.

RECOMMENDATION: C. K. Barrett has written the commentary par excellence; it is difficult to see how it could be improved, even though Conzelmann's book is bigger and more detailed.

8. II CORINTHIANS

Paul's second letter to the Corinthians can claim at least one distinction in the history of commenting: it is both the paradise and the despair of the commentator. No other New Testament book is in need of such careful exposition. It is necessary to set the scene and elucidate—as far as is possible at this time of day—Paul's tempestuous dealings with the Corinthian congregation. The value of II Corinthians to both ministers and people is self-evident, and it has a special claim on the thoughtful pastor who is searching for his or her job description as a "minister of the new covenant" and an agent of "reconciliation"—both key terms in this epistle. And, to cap it all, we may add C. K. Barrett's judgment in his standard commentary in the *Harper-Black* series that II Corinthians is the most difficult of all Paul's letters, yet at the same time this epistle contains "the fullest and most passionate account of what Paul meant by apostleship" and so what he regarded as central to ministry (p. 53).

Ministers of the word, therefore, need positive and practical help in this field. We can be thankful that it is forthcoming. C. K. Barrett's commentary and James Denney's treatment in *The Expositor's Bible* (old in years, but remarkably fresh and apropos on many issues) form an unbeatable combination. The recommendations that follow are a supplement to this duo, not a substitute for it.

Jean Héring has a sprightly written effort and many a serendipitous aside to brighten the landscape of a serious work. For instance, there is the obvious shift in mood from ch. 9 to ch. 10 of II Corinthians, a break all the commentators observe. Only Héring knows how to put it in a *mot juste:* "A complete change of scene. Titus and the Macedonians have disappeared, along with the collection-plates." We recommend this volume, which is, of course, the English translation of his *CNT* edition.

Of more pedestrian character and marked by scholarly evenhandedness (sometimes of the heavy type) is Philip E. Hughes (*NICNT*). But there is some excellent writing here, and a broad set of options is offered (see, e.g., on Paul's thorn in 12:1–10). R. V. G. Tasker's *Tyndale* volume is much slighter and somewhat disappointing, especially when set side by side with Richard P. C. Hanson's equally slender, but more nuanced, contribution to the *Torch* series. Not to be missed are the exceptional part-volumes on this epistle, that by Murray J. Harris in *The Expositor's Bible Commentary* (an otherwise undistinguished series, I fear), and the earlier work of George R. Beasley-Murray in *The Broadman Bible Commentary,* Vol. 11.

F. F. Bruce (*NCB*) is hampered by space restriction, but packs a lot of muscle into a few pages. R. H. Strachan (*Moffatt*) only occasionally shines, which is hard to believe, since he is commenting on Moffatt's vivid translation, itself as good as any commentary. J. H. Bernard (*Expositor's Greek Testament*) is old-fashioned and now antiquated, yet we still await its replacement as a serviceable commentary on the Greek text.

European contributions include Lietzmann-Kümmel (*HzNT*) which lacks a corresponding English version; and then there are erudite studies by Rudolf Bultmann (on the entire epistle) and Ernst Käsemann (on chs. 10–13), still untranslated. But their insights are to be seen in such modern English works as Barrett.

RECOMMENDATION: In terms of a sympathetic understanding of Paul's pastoral dealings with the Corinthian situations, Denney offers the most suggestive treatment. But Barrett cannot be edged out and is indispensable for getting a handle on the modern discussion of II Corinthians.

9. GALATIANS

Our choice for Galatians falls on two works, each representing a distinctive contribution to this lively epistle whose understanding is so important and central in our quest for the historical Paul. J. B. Lightfoot's commentary (1865, reprinted in 1950) may seem to be hopelessly dated, given its appearance over a century ago. In point of fact, it is one of those timeless commentaries which will never go out of date. As a piece of solid exegetical scholarship, based on the Greek text, it remains unsurpassed, and I have found myself turning to it repeatedly.

At the opposite end, Hans-Dieter Betz's recent contribution to *Hermeneia* addresses a different set of issues from that of Lightfoot, but always with the same rigor of scholarship that characterizes the earlier work. For those who may feel intimidated by Betz's severely academic and literary approach (see John Bligh, *Galatians,* for this enterprise carried to an extreme), let me mention F. F. Bruce's title in the new *NIGTC* series. Once more we are indebted to Bruce's historical exegesis, strongly in the Protestant-evangelical tradition, and well designed to guide the reader to the heart of Paul's teaching on the gospel. Ragnar Bring, *Commentary on Galatians,* is theologically oriented in the direction of Lutheran dogmatics. These three or four volumes all complement one another, and a case could be made for including each of them in any minister's library.

E. D. Burton in the *ICC* can now be safely passed over, as indeed can Herman N. Ridderbos in *NICNT*. Both were useful in their day, but are now superseded by more recent studies.

What is good about G. S. Duncan in the *Moffatt* series is the clarity of his exposition and the helpfulness of his lucid writing. So I would commend it to any who need an easy-to-read book, which makes no demands on our knowledge of

Greek, yet gets to the heart of Paul's message. Less successful is Donald Guthrie's volume in *NCB;* it lacks any distinctive appeal or interest, which is a pity, since Galatians needed a strong contribution in this series. The bibliographies are deficient, and the book lacks sparkle. R. Alan Cole in *Tyndale* writes in a workmanlike way, but no remarkable feature distinguishes this work either.

On the other hand, I have found William Neil's contribution in the *Cambridge Bible Commentary* to be an incisive treatment, though in small compass. An older, slender book by Handley C. G. Moule, *The Cross and the Spirit*, is full of good things, extremely suggestive to the preacher. On a broader front, Charles Cousar in the *Interpretation* series writes with preachers particularly in mind, and does a creditable job. His book augurs well for the new John Knox series, in which it appears as the first New Testament title.

Since Galatians contains some themes central to the Pauline gospel, we should also include a few titles that devote themselves to matters such as "righteousness," "justification," "faith," and "covenant." Pride of place goes to John Reumann's extended essay *Righteousness in the New Testament*, with comments by two Catholic scholars, Joseph A. Fitzmyer and Jerome D. Quinn. Reumann's writing is top-notch and every preacher owes it to himself or herself to wrestle with this superb piece of biblical exegesis. J. A. Ziesler, *The Meaning of Righteousness in Paul*, is also fine and worth close attention, along with M. T. Brauch's contribution to E. P. Sanders, *Paul and Palestinian Judaism*, in which he surveys recent European scholarship on "righteousness" and "justification" in a deft manner.

We lack a recent monograph on "faith" in Paul, at least in English. There is a good German treatment by Hermann Binder, *Der Glaube bei Paulus*; and we need to go back to earlier studies by W. H. P. Hatch (1925) or better, H. Ljungman, *Pistis: A Study of Its Presuppositions and Its Meaning in Pauline Use* (1964). Otto Michel in *NIDNTT* is disappointingly thin, and could well have been augmented in the English translation. "Covenant" fares little better for monograph treatment, with Delbert R. Hillers' *Covenant: The History of a Biblical Idea* virtually unchallenged in this field.

RECOMMENDATION: It is a difficult choice between Betz and Bruce, if our interest is in exegetical precision. Both have a lot to offer and nicely complement each other.

10. EPHESIANS

The exegetical issues thrown up by the text of Ephesians are most fully covered by Markus Barth's painstakingly thorough two-volume work (*AB*). But his smaller book *The Broken Wall* should not be missed, as it offers a scintillating treatment of what Ephesians as a document of Christian unity is all about. A companion volume would be John A. Mackay, *God's Order.* Yet these two shorter books are not exegetical studies; rather, they give broad overviews of what to look for in studying and communicating the message of Ephesians.

For practical purposes, preachers will find much help in the briefer treatment given by C. Leslie Mitton in *NCB*, the best up-to-date commentary in small compass. Any point not dealt with by Mitton will appear in Francis W. Beare's well-written contribution to *The Interpreter's Bible*. Both Mitton and Beare assume a post-Pauline author. If Ephesians is to be regarded as "the crown of Paulinism" (in C. H. Dodd's phrase in *The Abingdon Bible Commentary*), Ernest F. Scott (*Moffatt*) and Francis Foulkes (*Tyndale*) may be appealed to—but their exegetical worth is not remarkable and they offer little to the preacher. The issues are really settled by one's attitude to Ernst Käsemann's thesis that this New Testament letter reflects early Catholic tendencies. His essay in *Studies in Luke-Acts*, edited by Leander E. Keck and J. Louis Martyn, is worth consulting as one that broke new ground and asked some innovative questions.

To appreciate Ephesians in the light of a post-Pauline situation at a time when the church was facing problems of Israel's disappearance from the scene and grappling with the onset of Gnostic influence, as well as becoming preoccupied with the role of an institutional ministry and a growing creedalism, we need the help of the Europeans. The mainstay here is Joachim Gnilka's incisive commentary (*Herder*, in German). Heinrich Schlier's commentary (also in German) reflects the attempt to accommodate "early Catholic" traits within the Roman obedience, and marks the author's pilgrimage from Bultmannian Protestantism to that church home. Nonetheless, Schlier's work is full of insights that deserve a wider audience in the English-speaking world.

For a comparable work in English we shall await Andrew T. Lincoln's full-scale commentary on the Greek text (*WBC*, forthcoming). On the other hand, E. K. Simpson's eccentric contribution to *NICNT*, issued in 1957, can only be regarded as a lost opportunity. F. F. Bruce's commentary in 1961 was meant for popular consumption, and we understand that his revision of Simpson's work will represent a notable advance. Some reference to other literature on Ephesians may be seen in my contribution to the *Broadman Bible Commentary*, Vol. 11.

More popular works are offered by J. A. Allan (*Torch*) and G. H. P. Thompson (*Cambridge Bible Commentary*). But neither is really significant. Dale Moody's *The Hope of Glory* is more replete with insight for preachers.

Students of Greek will find J. Armitage Robinson's edition indispensable, even if the exegetical help has to be teased out. More direct and immediate help is provided by Charles Masson's commentary (in *CNT*), requiring only a minimal knowledge of Greek and written in simple French (as yet untranslated, a neglect that is hardly credible, considering the dearth of really good commentaries on Ephesians that are neither too technical nor too unhelpfully brief and oversimplified). This is our number-one recommendation—if only the language barrier can be surmounted.

Edgar J. Goodspeed in his scholarly lifetime made a distinctive contribution to the study of Ephesians. His *The Meaning of Ephesians* sought to provide a key to the enigma of this New Testament document; and irrespective of his particular solution, his words are still worth weighing. The same goes for J. C. Kirby's *Ephesians: Baptism and Pentecost*, a book that was one of the first to bring liturgical studies to bear upon this letter, with fruitful results.

Two titles, precisely look-alike, have put together abbreviated commentaries on the four so-termed prison epistles (Ephesians, Philippians, Colossians, Philemon). Both are well-written and, as far as they go, excellent value in small space, but the space limitation naturally precludes any extended treatments. They are: J. Leslie Houlden, *Paul's Letters from Prison (Pelican)* and George B. Caird, *Paul's Letters from Prison (New Clarendon Bible)*.

RECOMMENDATION: A firm choice is not easy because the field is so limited. Barth's is the fullest offering, but Mitton is not to be disdained.

11. PHILIPPIANS

Our first resource for Philippians has to be J. B. Lightfoot, whose Macmillan commentary, written in the late nineteenth century and reprinted in our day, still remains a model of what a commentary on a Pauline epistle should be. Based on the Greek text, it still retains its unique place in spite of recent advances in Pauline studies, which chiefly concern the nature of the opposition in ch. 3, and the Christological-soteriological meaning of the "odyssey of Christ" passage in 2:6–11.

Francis W. Beare represents a thoroughly modern approach to what, in some ways, is the simplest of the apostle's letters and for that reason is often turned to by pastorally-minded preachers in search of a case-study approach to their pulpit ministry.

In shorter compass, my own effort in *NCB* tries to set the letter in the midst of the contemporary debate. An early commentary of mine in the *Tyndale* series sought to be more popular and to expound the letter for the minister and Bible class teacher, with an occasional glance at leading critical issues. J. H. Michael (*Moffatt*) has more space to achieve this goal. Michael has several good sermon illustrations and writes attractively with a pastor's needs in view.

The most recent full-scale commentary is one that also fills the spot for a five-star recommendation. I refer to Jean-François Collange's 1973 contribution to *CNT*, which is available in English. The volume it replaced, written by Pierre Bonnard, was itself a notable volume in the French series but never translated. Collange has brought a bevy of fresh insights to Philippian studies, and his work can be warmly recommended as a mine of information and inspiration for the preacher's study.

If we turn to books in smaller format, a close rival would be J. L. Houlden's *Paul's Letters from Prison (Pelican)*, which includes other so-called "captivity letters" assigned to Paul. Houlden's space is limited, but he makes every paragraph count. Of similar format is George B. Caird, *Paul's Letters from Prison (New Clarendon Bible)*, but, if I mistake not, this book lacks flair as it seeks to unfold Paul's pastoral writings to the Gentile churches. The traditionalist stance of the commentator may have something to do with it, and one has only to set it over against Collange's commentary, with all its Gallic verve and élan, to see the difference. Gerald F. Hawthorne's commentary on the Greek text (*WBC*) will press all these previous studies into service in a notable work of interest to those who have at least a minimal knowledge of the original Greek.

We turn now to much slighter works, for which there is a ready market among those who need a quick-reference type of commentary: F. C. Synge's *Torch* volume and Kenneth Grayston's two volumes, one in the *Cambridge Bible Commentary*, the other in *Epworth Preacher's Commentaries*. These titles serve their (limited) purpose, though preachers should beware of relying exclusively on them. Karl Barth's brief exposition, *The Epistle to the Philippians*, gives a distillation of what Paul would have said had he studied at Basel! But it makes entertaining and informative reading for all that.

Older works of note—H. A. A. Kennedy (*Expositor's Greek Testament*), and Handley C. G. Moule, as well as J. J. Müller (*NICNT*) and M. R. Vincent (*ICC*)—are all severely dated by now and are useful for an occasional classical reference, but they do not grapple with the leading issues in modern understanding of Paul's pastoral concerns at Philippi.

Foreign-language books will hardly appeal to the hard-pressed preacher in this field. Ernst Lohmeyer remains a classic in the *MeyerK* series, revised but left largely intact by Werner Schmauch's revision. Full of insight is Gerhard Friedrich's much briefer treatment (*NTD*), and this can be relied on for helpful suggestions if the German language is no hindrance. I found Wilhelm Michaelis (*Theologischer Handkommentar*) exactly what the series promised, a theological exposition at a deeply satisfying level. Again a recommendation is given, if the untranslated book poses no problem.

Many a preacher will want at some time to try his or her hand at exegeting Phil. 2:6–11, especially at Advent or in Holy Week. Most of the titles above give ample space to this difficult yet rewarding hymnic passage, particularly Collange and Hawthorne. My own *Carmen Christi*, devoted to a history and exegesis of these six verses and their varied understanding in the modern Christological debate, is available in a revised form (1983).

RECOMMENDATION: Collange is a clear leader in a crowded field, with Beare close behind and Hawthorne at his heels.

12. COLOSSIANS AND PHILEMON

There is an embarrassment of riches where recent commentaries on Colossians are concerned. Eduard Schweizer's work *The Letter to the Colossians*, newly rendered from the German edition of *EKK*, is self-recommending, and those who know Schweizer's gift for down-to-earth exegesis and are familiar with the notable array of scholarly studies on Colossians already published by him will not be disappointed in this significant contribution. His text has a number of telling illustrations that can easily find their way into sermons.

Less popularly presented but also resting on exact exegetical research is Peter T. O'Brien (*WBC*). It is based on the Greek text and steers a middle course through the minefield of such debated matters as the authorship and the setting of the letter, yet with a full discussion of the pros and cons. In this Colossians volume, Philemon is also included, with some helpful essays on the reason for that letter's being sent.

At an even more rigorous level of scholarship is Eduard Lohse's *Hermeneia* commentary on both epistles. Obviously the preacher will have to thread his or her way through a labyrinth of data to get to the heart of the text, but the exercise is well worth while and will repay dividends in the pulpit once the material is suitably digested and refashioned for public presentation.

If Lohse and O'Brien will make us work at our Greek, help is at hand in Charles F. D. Moule's commentary (*Cambridge Greek Testament*), which has become a minor classic in its own right and shows a master exegete at work. For those needing plainer fare we recommend F. F. Bruce (*NICNT*), coupled with E. K. Simpson on Ephesians, but as different from that half-volume as it is possible to imagine. Even more straightforward and with application to the preacher's task is my own *Colossians: The Church's Lord and the Christian's Liberty*, due for a reprint soon.

Smaller commentaries on both letters include my contribution to *NCB*, with a bibliography up to 1981 in the latest edition; Herbert Carson's treatment in the *Tyndale* series; and the commentaries covering the prison epistles by G. H. P. Thompson, J. L. Houlden, and George B. Caird (see on Ephesians and Philippians, above). William Barclay's volume in his one-person series (*Daily Study Bible*) is one of the most successful in that comprehensive set, and I have used it with great profit when a telling illustration or an illuminating word study is called for.

To see what lies behind the text and situation of Colossians we can find a wealth of detail in essays ranging from J. B. Lightfoot (whose commentary, in its reprinted 1879 edition, is still valuable) to Günther Bornkamm (who wrote in a ground-breaking way on the error underlying the Colossian "philosophy," Col. 2:8). These have been collected by Fred O. Francis and Wayne A. Meeks under the title *Conflict at Colossae*. This unusual volume is for serious students and teachers, though pastors could not fail to profit from these perceptive essays. The essay from Martin Dibelius makes handily available the heart of his commentary in *HzNT*.

A commentary with a shorter scope is Hans Conzelmann's contribution in *NTD*; it has, however, not been translated. It is full of pithy comments and authoritative judgments on some difficult texts in Colossians.

On *Philemon* we draw attention to John Knox's provocative study, *Philemon Among the Letters of Paul*, whose second edition in 1959 brought up to date an earlier work that put Philemon "on the map," as it were, and offered new insights into the character and purpose of this much-neglected part of the Pauline library.

RECOMMENDATION: On the Greek text, yet with every help given to the Greekless reader, O'Brien is probably best, with a different approach evident in Lohse.

13. I AND II THESSALONIANS

The most serviceable commentary on the Thessalonian letters has until recently been Ernest Best (*Harper-Black*), and this title has many virtues, not least that it is easy to consult and full of scholarly wisdom, theological insight, pastoral interest, and plain sense. As an admirable supplement, at a level that introduces Greek as the basis of the comment, we salute F. F. Bruce's recent full-scale commentary (*WBC*). His work is marked by customary thoroughness and attention to detail, especially in setting the epistles against their contemporary background. There are some valuable introductory sections and an interesting excursus on "The Antichrist." An even more extensive work on these letters has been announced: Karl P. Donfried in the new *ICC*.

At the level of more compact works, preachers have had to be content with two titles by Leon Morris (one in *NICNT* and a simpler version in *Tyndale*: both are very useful, however). Less useful is A. L. Moore (*NCB*), a volume now replaced by a newly written commentary by I. Howard Marshall, who has considerably more space at his disposal than his predecessor had. Denys E. H. Whiteley (*New Clarendon Bible*) is a smallish work, and is consequently hampered. But Whiteley's approach, both theological and historical, is helpful, as is William Neil's *Moffatt* contribution, now showing signs of age.

Even more popular is Ronald A. Ward's volume, written with preachers and expositors in mind; and D. E. Hiebert's work is similarly oriented.

There are older books that can often yield hidden treasures if we are prepared to dig. Outstanding in this category is James Denney (*Expositor's Bible*), with other places taken by E. J. Bicknell (*Westminster*) and J. E. Frame (*ICC*).

In the European languages, pride of place goes certainly to Béda Rigaux (*EB*), a masterly work at every level, but not translated from French. Another very serviceable volume, also in French, is Charles Masson (*CNT*), whose brief comments are always worth noting.

The *MeyerK* volume is by Ernst von Dobschütz, but is now dated; and Martin Dibelius in *HzNT* is a pre-World War II study. For the latest trends, including the idea of the Thessalonian church as racked by Gnostic teaching, we turn to Willi Marxsen (on I Thessalonians in the series *Zürcher Bibelkommentar*; a companion volume on II Thessalonians is advertised). Schmithals' chapter on the Thessalonian church in his *Paul and the Gnostics* points in the direction these commentaries take.

Charles H. Giblin, *The Threat to Faith*, is a painstaking exegetical examination of II Thessalonians 2, a source of much puzzlement (and wild speculation) among preachers and popular teachers.

RECOMMENDATION: The most useful commentary overall is that by Best, with Bruce and Marshall bringing the discussion up to date.

14. I AND II TIMOTHY AND TITUS

The three short pastoral epistles, ostensibly addressed to Timothy and Titus, pose their own problems of interpretation. For one thing, the general name by which they have been known since the last century is confusing. They are less "pastoral" than directed to the ordering of congregational life; and they represent a period of church history when the visible structures of the church, including the ministry, various offices, and a rudimentary church "order" were becoming important.

Commentaries that will be of greatest benefit are surely those that address the prime issue of the "life setting," even if no final solution is likely. That is why the little part-volume by Reginald H. Fuller in the *Proclamation Commentaries* series is an excellent starter. C. K. Barrett (*New Clarendon Bible*) is more ambitious in commenting on the Greek text; but the more immediately serviceable is J. L. Houlden (*Pelican*), who can be relied on to give us orientation, an asset especially needful in exegeting these books.

From this we graduate to larger works. J. N. D. Kelly (*Harper-Black*) is full of good things, traditional and comprehensive, with Walter Lock (*ICC*) now dated but a repository of timeless observations. The classic volume is C. Spicq (*EB*), but it remains untranslated.

Also untranslated is Joachim Jeremias' interesting contribution in *NTD*, which, while arguing for the essentially Pauline character of the letters, is flexible in recognizing several other influences of various kinds, including the use of an amanuensis to give the letters their final shape. Lacking that flexibility is Donald Guthrie (*Tyndale*), who makes the pastorals a test case for his understanding of why pseudonymous attributions are to be rejected. But evangelicals (e.g., Arthur G. Patzia, "The Deutero-Pauline Hypothesis: An Attempt at Clarification," *The Evangelical Quarterly*, 1980) are less intransigent than they used to be, and the debate has lost much of its fire and relevance.

At the opposite end of the spectrum from Guthrie, whose commentary still retains value with a clear expounding of Paul in a situationless way, is Burton Scott Easton's book *The Pastoral Epistles*. Written with zest and admirable clarity, it posits a non-Pauline author ("the Pastor") and has valuable studies on word lists and ethical norms that seem to Easton to require a development in the church's handling of ethical issues at a time later than Paul.

Anthony T. Hanson (*Cambridge Bible Commentary*) has both a slender commentary and a more valuable independent book of exegetical studies on the crucial passages in these letters, and in this area of few serious helps this title (*Studies in the Pastoral Epistles*) may be warmly greeted. Stephen G. Wilson has some useful insights in his book *Luke and the Pastoral Epistles*, in which he attempts to show the connection between Luke and the writer of these letters.

For the Greek exegete there is the work of Martin Dibelius, revised by Hans Conzelmann, contributed to *HzNT*. This joint effort is now available in translation in the *Hermeneia* series. It is an indispensable resource volume of parallels, allusions, and data on the history of exegesis. But it probably is too full for the pastor's immediate needs. The other commentary based on the Greek is that of E. K. Simpson, a wayward volume, full of linguistic echoes and allusions across the entire range of Greek literature, Attic and Hellenistic. But it fails as an attempt to pierce to the theological concerns of the author and his *Sitz im Leben*. We still await a really satisfying treatment of the pastorals.

RECOMMENDATION: No commentary presents itself as clearly the leader. Houlden offers great insight within a restricted compass.

15. Hebrews

In many ways, Hebrews also stands in need of a really first-rate commentary if it is to yield its deepest treasures. The best treatments enable us to get inside the author's mind and see his (or her!) church problems through a prism that to modern readers appears strange and forbidding.

It is a toss-up between F. F. Bruce (*NICNT*) and Hugh Montefiore (*Harper-Black*), both of comparable dimension and scope and both nearly twenty years old. Both are well-written, to be sure, with Montefiore somewhat more appealing in layout and style and more provocative. Bruce has more data on display, writes cautiously, and is more useful in the long term.

The commentary of Philip E. Hughes is in the conservative tradition held by Bruce, but with less interest in lexical matters. The theology of Hebrews is expounded in solid Reformed fashion.

George W. Buchanan (*AB*) is best described as unusual and idiosyncratic, so while it stimulates it rarely satisfies. Which is a pity, since it was scheduled to appear at a time when a first-class commentary of Hebrews was demanded. The shorter work of Jean Héring, translated from *CNT*, is full of excellent ideas and suggestions toward a sound exegesis, and preachers will be grateful to have it at hand.

Preachers will value the *multum in parvo* quality of William Barclay on Hebrews (*Daily Study Bible*), hailed as the best thing written in that justly praised series from his industrious pen. Barclay's interest in Philo and Hellenistic Greek was called into play and used to great—and practical—effect.

For serious students intent on exploring the Greek text in depth there are C. Spicq's two volumes, but in French. Of equal weight theologically is Otto Michel's commentary (*MeyerK* series) in German. Both will enrich our understanding once the language barrier is crossed.

Of older substantial works, James Moffatt in *ICC* has stood

the test of time and is probably due for honorable retirement.
B. F. Westcott also was valuable in its day, but Moffatt and
Westcott (and we should add, William Manson's excellent
study *The Epistle to the Hebrews*) were all written in the pre-
Qumran era and so are antiquated when it comes to the
meaning of Hebrews 1, 2, and 7, to take only selected
themes. Studies on the role of Melchizedek, for example,
have been much in prominence, as in Fred L. Horton, *The
Melchizedek Tradition*, and Philo's ghost still haunts the scene,
where the best guide is Ronald Williamson, *Philo and the
Epistle to the Hebrews.*

Of smaller proportions, Thomas Hewitt's book (*Tyndale*)
was a disappointment from its publication and, we hear, is to
be replaced and not simply revised. Theodore H. Robinson
(*Moffatt*) also must receive a similar negative verdict, though
at least one other Old Testament scholar, A. B. Davidson, has
written on Hebrews and produced a notable exposition.

Devotionally (and homiletically) we have found great value
in Andrew Murray, *The Holiest of All*, though it has a distinct
doctrinal bias in the direction of "higher life" teaching. A
more up-to-date homiletical study is that of Raymond Brown.
More critically oriented, yet with value to the preacher, is
Robert Jewett's recent work.

RECOMMENDATION: Bruce's work is solid and expository,
with Héring bringing in some European studies.

16. I PETER

Studies in I Peter took a decisive turn with the appearance
of E. G. Selwyn's massive contribution to the Macmillan
series in 1946. Prior to that, critical commentaries of note
were those by C. A. Bigg (*ICC*), James Moffatt in the *Moffatt*
series, and F. J. A. Hort (his commentary went as far as 2:17).
The first and the last of these were based on the Greek text,
but at a stroke they were all superseded by Selwyn's magisterial work, also on the Greek.

Within a short time Francis W. Beare came along in 1947

to challenge as though by prescience Selwyn's work in matters of authorship (by denying Petrine authorship), dating (by placing the letter in the early second century), and details of exegesis. Beare's third edition (1970) shows the influence of the later Continental work, particularly that of Windisch-Preisker (*HzNT*) in the area of a putative liturgical origin of the letter, but Beare is cautious in accepting these proposals.

For the latest treatment of I Peter, which also opened a new era in registering the effect of the sociological study of this kind of literature and its interpretation, we must turn to Leonhard Goppelt (*MeyerK*). Goppelt's work is marked by thoroughness, as befits its place in the German series, but it has already proved a path breaker in provoking further studies on the social significance of Peter's readership as a disadvantaged group who needed to discover their true identity as the people and family of God. John H. Elliott's title, *A Home for the Homeless*, accurately denotes this newest trend in Petrine studies, and equally carves out a distinctive place for Petrine Christianity in the New Testament churchly literature. No longer can we subsume Peter under Paul's aegis. James D. G. Dunn's *Unity and Diversity in the New Testament* (sec. 76) shows how this "discovery" of Peter as a "bridge-man," holding together extreme positions in apostolic literature, can be turned to good use, contributing to our awareness of New Testament Christianity as essentially pluriform and multifaceted.

In smaller compass we must give highest praise to Charles E. B. Cranfield's commentary as a veritable gold mine of exegetical insight and help for the preacher's task. Close partners are Alan M. Stibbs (*Tyndale*) and Ernest Best (*NCB*). The latter is the fullest of the smaller commentaries and replete with exegetical value and practical help.

In terms of overall serviceability and for the purpose of getting to the heart of Peter's message, J. N. D. Kelly (*Harper-Black*) is without peer. Whenever we have consulted him, he has unfailingly produced the goods, even if his work needs to be supplemented by the larger books mentioned earlier.

Bo Reicke (*AB*) is unfortunate in trying to achieve too much in a restricted space. J. W. C. Wand (*Westminster*) is now dated and can safely be passed over. At the opposite end of the spectrum in terms of their completeness and treatment of all the issues provoked by a particular text are to be mentioned K. H. Schelkle (*Herder*) and C. Spicq (in the series *Sources Bibliques*). The latter has excellent linguistic notes.

However, hard-pressed expositors have all they need in the quartet of Selwyn, Beare, Kelly, and Best, as indicated. To enliven many a sermon on I Peter, I have found William Barclay's *Daily Study Bible* excellent in giving fine word studies and apt illustrations drawn from the ancient world.

Larger monographs such as Elliott (*A Home for the Homeless*; see also his earlier work on 2:1–10, *The Elect and the Holy*); David L. Balch (on the household code teaching, *Let Wives Be Submissive*); and William J. Dalton, *Christ's Proclamation to the Spirits* concentrate on special issues, and it is good to know where to turn for extra help. A conspectus of significant studies on I Peter is given in John H. Elliott's essay "The Rehabilitation of an Exegetical Step-Child: 1 Peter in Recent Research," *Journal of Biblical Literature*, 1976.

RECOMMENDATION: If Goppelt gets translated into English, it will clearly lead the field. Until then, Selwyn is dependable but dated, and Kelly is a multipurpose work.

17. JAMES

Luther's negative assessment that James's epistle is really "an epistle of straw" compared to other New Testament books (e.g., Romans, Galatians, Ephesians, and I Peter, "which show us Christ and urge us to him") is well known and unfortunate. The Reformer's further remark that "there is nothing of the nature of the gospel about it" says as much about Luther's understanding of the gospel as it does about the value of this enigmatic epistle.

Commentaries, therefore, that take James seriously and not dismissively are the ones to be most welcomed. There is much to encourage preachers to see James as a piece of New Testament hortatory literature (the merit of Martin Dibelius' commentary in the *Hermeneia* series—where it is available in an English translation—is that is shows this genre clearly). Two recent large-scale attempts to interpret James against the background of Jewish Christianity are Peter H. Davids (in *NIGTC*) and Sophie Laws (*Harper-Black*), the former placing James in the social setting of Jewish messianists in the 50s and early 60s, the latter emphasizing the possibility of a Roman origin of the tract. James B. Adamson's volume (*NICNT*), which stressed Hellenistic elements in the epistle, is disappointing, and is now superseded by Davids and Laws, as Adamson's commentary in turn took the place of Alexander Ross in the *NICNT* series. The discoveries at Nag Hammadi, which included several tractates having to do with James's role, have given a fresh impetus to the study of Jewish Christianity, thus antiquating several older commentaries.

The Davids volume uses Greek. Students of that language can turn with profit to an older work, that of James B. Mayor, recently reprinted, which with F. J. A. Hort and John H. Ropes (*ICC*) lays a strong foundation in classical and Hellenistic parallels. Hort's work covers the text as far as 4:7.

More popular commentaries are Bo Reicke (*AB*), E. M. Sidebottom (*NCB*) and R. V. G. Tasker (*Tyndale*). The most suggestive for the preacher's use, however, is C. Leslie Mitton's commentary, an independent work that seeks to bring out James's message for Palestinian believers, with a modern application.

More scholarly contributions, available to readers of European languages, are Franz Mussner (*Herder*) and Hans Windisch (*HzNT*). The former is more helpful in leading to the theological message of James. Joseph Chaine's work in the *Etudes Bibliques* series well maintains the rigorous, thoroughgoing emphasis in that collection; Jean Cantinat (also in French) is a briefer treatment (in *Sources Bibliques*).

G. H. Rendall's study should not be overlooked, since he anticipated in his day some of the more exciting trends in the modern appreciation of James. Of sermonic character are J. Alec Motyer, *The Tests of Faith*; D. E. Hiebert, *The Epistle of James* (with a fine bibliography); and David A. Hubbard, *The Book of James: Wisdom That Works*; with William Barclay's volume (*Daily Study Bible*) speaking also directly to the preacher's interest.

RECOMMENDATION: Davids is the most recent and the best so far, with Laws a close second.

18. II PETER AND JUDE

Second Peter and Jude are rather neglected parts of the New Testament and have not drawn much attention, often being lumped together indifferently with the more appealing First Peter. So we have composite works by Charles E. B. Cranfield (*Torch*), James Moffatt (*Moffatt* series) and Bo Reicke (*AB*). E. M. Sidebottom combines II Peter and Jude in *NCB*, but limitation of space is a severe drawback. E. Michael B. Green comments on the two epistles in *Tyndale*, and at a popular level this choice is made in default of much else of note. The conservative stance of Green is well known. J. N. D. Kelly (*Harper-Black*) is more thorough, and his attractive work on II Peter is warmly recommended as open to all the arguments that bear on the setting of this epistle, its language problems, and the type of false teaching it opposes.

Much more satisfying than all previous publications, however, is the new work of Richard J. Bauckham (*WBC*), based on the Greek text, but written to ensure a wide appeal. It breaks fresh ground as to life setting and theological emphasis by utilizing some recent Continental studies, e.g., Tord Fornberg's *An Early Church in a Pluralistic Society*, and some important literary finds. Important Gnostic studies from the Nag Hammadi library and Jewish pseudepigraphical books are pressed into service.

Also available on the Greek text is James B. Mayor's mammoth work, recently reprinted. But it is antiquated, with the result that our interest in these documents is hardly sustained. The same verdict goes for C. A. Bigg (*ICC*) and J. W. C. Wand (*Westminster*).

Foreign language commentaries of note are K. H. Schelkle (*Herder*) and Walter Grundmann (*Theologischer Handkommentar*). But these are now superseded by Bauckham's work, mentioned earlier—a rare tribute to an English-speaking study that is now an international front-runner.

RECOMMENDATION: There is no doubt that Bauckham is the choice for detailed exegesis and assistance to the preacher.

19. I, II, AND III JOHN

The recent exposition of I. Howard Marshall on the three epistles of John (*NICNT*) summarizes a lot of previous scholarship and may head the list of recommendations, paired now with the exhaustive contribution to the *Anchor Bible* series by Raymond E. Brown. Thus, preachers have these ample resources where, until fairly recently, there was little to improve on B. F. Westcott's commentary written on the Greek text (recently reprinted) or C. H. Dodd's classic in *Moffatt.* J. L. Houlden (*Harper-Black*) is a commentary simpler than all of these, yet going to the heart of the exegetical task.

In smaller compass, yet with great penetration to John's pastoral thought, is John R. W. Stott's volume in the *Tyndale* series, which probably will meet the needs of those hard pressed to get quickly to the center of an often deceptively simple body of New Testament writings.

At the other extreme, Rudolf Bultmann's volume (English translation in *Hermeneia*) is for scholars and students.

Three more popular approaches may be unreservedly commended, since two of them have stood the test of many years' use and the third is excellent for its limpid style. They are: Robert Law, *The Tests of Life* (a devotional classic and a seed plot of many sermons, I should suppose); G. G. Findlay, *Fellowship in the Life Eternal*; and F. F. Bruce, *The Epistles of John.*

Other books in this area are important for background reading. High on the list is Raymond E. Brown's *Community of the Beloved Disciple* for an intriguing exercise in literary detective work, with a special value for exegesis. Additional titles on the Johannine community have been mentioned under the Gospel of John.

RECOMMENDATION: Brown (*AB*) is the fullest and the most recommendable, though older titles such as Law and Findlay ought not to be passed over in the quest for sermonic guides.

20. REVELATION

Commentaries on the unusual book of Revelation have a value directly determined by the author's starting point and presuppositions. The litmus test, it seems to me, is whether such an author has really grappled with the genre of The Revelation to John as apocalyptic. It would be a salutary exercise for any would-be preacher who elects to expose his or her congregation to the intricacies of Revelation to read some scholarly account of what apocalyptic, Jewish and Christian, is and is not. We recommend David S. Russell's *The Method and Message of Jewish Apocalyptic*, or George W. E. Nickelsburg, *Jewish Literature Between the Bible and the Mishnah.* Failing this discipline, Klaus Koch's *The Rediscovery of Apocalyptic* or (a simpler treatment) Leon Morris' *Apocalyptic* should be required and propaedeutic reading. A larger book, *The Open Heaven*, by Christopher Rowland, is a ground breaker and makes fascinating reading.

With this preamble, we can simply pass by a host of popular, fanciful, and misrepresenting treatments, of which perhaps Hal Lindsey's titles are the most ubiquitous. J.

Christiaan Beker's *Paul's Apocalyptic Gospel* and Robert Jew-ett's *Jesus Against the Rapture* are useful antidotes.

We certainly do not urge that the Apocalypse should not be taken seriously, or that its message is not truly Christian. George R. Beasley-Murray's richly suggestive volume in *NCB* is admirable in that connection, bringing out the Christian significance of the text, whatever Jewish or pagan elements may lie in the background. A similar treatment is George B. Caird (*Harper-Black*). These two books are the preacher's main standbys, with more succinct writing to be found in Leon Morris (*Tyndale*) and more futurist eschatology in George E. Ladd. To know what scholarly study does with Revelation, we can keep Robert H. Mounce's erudite edition (*NICNT*) within reach. All these titles cover the same ground with considerable overlap, yet with varying degrees of detail. All, however, share a broadly similar hermeneutical approach and see the Apocalypse against its first-century Asia Minor background, yet with a message of timeless appeal and relevance to the church.

More eccentric is Josephine Massyngberde Ford (*AB*), but highly entertaining as a study. Also idiosyncratic is Austin M. Farrer, *The Rebirth of Images*, whose title speaks for itself as offering an interpretative key to the book's symbolism.

The average sermon is hardly likely to need the resources provided by R. H. Charles' magisterial two-volume work in *ICC*. And in a sense the work of Charles, an acknowledged expert in this field, need not be redone, so that·these books are monuments to learning and solid exegesis, but hardly calculated to lift the preacher's spirits. For that inspiration we recommend *The Lord Reigneth* by Adam W. Burnet.

For more immediate help we have on hand the following: for quick-reference needs, J. P. M. Sweet has written a commentary in the *Pelican* series that is short, but based on sound scholarship. Jacques Ellul gives us an individual treat-ment in his *Apocalypse*. And the one volume intended (and successfully, too) to set the preacher's imagination to work is the book by William Hendriksen, *More Than Conquerors*, an admirable study that unhappily was not matched by the same commentator's prolific effort to exegete other New Testament books.

Other well-regarded titles are Henry B. Swete on the Greek, Martin Kiddle in *Moffatt* (practical, yet verbose), and William Milligan in the *Expositor's Bible* series, which is of mixed quality and scarcely comes near the modern recent titles in value or usefulness. Michael Wilcock, *I Saw Heaven Opened*, is a fine treatment, thoroughly recommendable, a book that has not had the public attention it deserves.

RECOMMENDATION: A definitive choice is impossible, given the variety of approaches to this book. For those coming new to this biblical book we recommend Wilcock in spite of its slender dimension. Those wishing a more detailed treatment are advised to get Caird or Beasley-Murray.

Bibliography

(For each author with more than one title, books are arranged in order of publication date.)

Abbott-Smith, G. *A Manual Greek Lexicon of the New Testament.* 3d ed. Edinburgh: T. & T. Clark, 1937.

Achtemeier, Paul J. *Mark.* Proclamation Commentaries. Ed. by Gerhard Krodel. Philadelphia: Fortress Press, 1975.

Adamson, James B. *The Epistle of James.* NICNT. Grand Rapids: Wm. B. Eerdmans Publishing Co.; London: Marshall, Morgan & Scott, 1976.

Aharoni, Yohanan. *The Land of the Bible.* Tr. by A. F. Rainey. 2d ed. rev. and enl. London: Burns & Oates, 1979; Philadelphia: Westminster Press, 1980.

———, and Avi-Yonah, Michael. *The Macmillan Bible Atlas.* New York: Macmillan Co.; London: Collier-Macmillan, 1968.

Aland, Kurt, ed. *Synopsis Quattuor Evangeliorum.* 9th ed. Stuttgart: Deutsche Bibelstiftung, 1976. E.T. *Synopsis of the Four Gospels: Greek-English Edition of the Synopsis Quattuor Evangeliorum.* 3d ed. United Bible Societies, 1979.

———; Black, Matthew; Martini, Carlo M.; Metzger, Bruce M.; and Wikgren, Allen, eds. *The Greek New Testament.* 3d ed. New York: United Bible Societies, 1975.

Albright, William F., and Mann, Christopher S. *Matthew: Introduction, Translation and Notes.* AB. Garden City, N.Y.: Doubleday & Co., 1971.

Alexander, Joseph A. *The Gospel According to Matthew.* Philadelphia: Presbyterian Board of Education, 1860. Repr. Baker Book House, 1980.

Allan, John A. *The Epistle to the Ephesians: Introduction and Commentary.* Torch Bible Commentaries. London: SCM Press, 1958; New York: Macmillan Co., 1959.

Allmen, Jean-Jacques von, ed. *The Vocabulary of the Bible.* Tr. by P. J. Allcock et al. London: Lutterworth Press, 1958. Published by Oxford University Press, London, 1958, under the title *Companion to the Bible.*

Anderson, Hugh. *The Gospel of Mark.* NCB. London: Oliphants, 1976; Grand Rapids: Wm. B. Eerdmans Publishing Co., 1981.

Aune, David E., ed. *Jesus and the Synoptic Gospels.* Downers Grove, Ill.: Inter-Varsity Press, 1981.

Bachmann, H., and Slaby, H., eds. *Computer-Konkordanz zum Novum Testamentum Graece von Nestle-Aland, 26. Auflage, und zum Greek New Testament, 3rd ed.* Institut für neutestamentliche Textforschung und Rechenzentrum der Universität Münster. Berlin and New York: Walter de Gruyter, 1980.

Baird, William. *The Corinthian Church: A Biblical Approach to Urban Culture.* New York: Abingdon Press, 1964.

Balch, David L. *Let Wives Be Submissive: The Domestic Code in 1 Peter.* Chico, Calif.: Scholars Press, 1981.

Barber, Cyril J. *The Minister's Library.* 2 vols. Grand Rapids: Baker Book House, 1974, 1983.

Barclay, William. *The Letters to the Philippians, Colossians, and Thessalonians: Translated with Introductions and Interpretations.* The Daily Study Bible. Rev. ed. Edinburgh: St. Andrews Press; Philadelphia: Westminster Press, 1975.

———. *The Letters of James and Peter: Translated with an Introduction and Interpretation.* The Daily Study Bible. Rev. ed. Edinburgh: St. Andrews Press; Philadelphia: Westminster Press, 1976.

———. *The Letter to the Hebrews: Translated with an Introduction and Interpretation.* The Daily Study Bible. Rev. ed.

Edinburgh: St. Andrews Press; Philadelphia: Westminster Press, 1976.

Barrett, Charles Kingsley, ed. *The New Testament Background: Selected Documents*. London: S.P.C.K., 1956; New York: Macmillan Co., 1957.

————. *A Commentary on the Epistle to the Romans*. HNTC. London: A. & C. Black, 1957; New York: Harper & Brothers, 1958.

————. *Luke the Historian in Recent Study*. London: Epworth Press, 1961. Repr. Philadelphia: Fortress Press, Facet Books, 1970.

————. *From First Adam to Last: A Study in Pauline Theology*. New York: Charles Scribner's Sons; London: A. & C. Black, 1962.

————. *The Pastoral Epistles in the New English Bible*. New Clarendon Bible. Oxford: Clarendon Press, 1963.

————. *Reading Through Romans*. London: Epworth Press, 1963; Philadelphia: Fortress Press, 1977.

————. *A Commentary on the First Epistle to the Corinthians*. HNTC. New York: Harper & Row; London: A. & C. Black, 1968.

————. *A Commentary on the Second Epistle to the Corinthians*. HNTC. London: A. & C. Black, 1973; New York: Harper & Row, 1974.

————. *The Gospel According to St. John: An Introduction with Commentary and Notes on the Greek Text*. London: S.P.C.K., 1955; 2d ed. 1978; Philadelphia: Westminster Press, 2d ed. 1978.

Barth, Karl. *The Epistle to the Romans* (1922). 6th ed. Tr. by Edwyn C. Hoskyns. London: Oxford University Press, 1933.

————. *A Shorter Commentary on Romans* (1919). Richmond: John Knox Press, 1959.

————. *The Epistle to the Philippians*. Tr. by James W. Leitch. Richmond: John Knox Press; London: SCM Press, 1962.

Barth, Markus. *The Broken Wall: A Study of the Epistle to the*

Ephesians. Philadelphia: Judson Press, 1959; London: William Collins Sons & Co., 1960.

————. *Ephesians: Introduction, Translation and Commentary.* AB. 2 vols. Garden City, N.Y.: Doubleday & Co., 1974.

Bauckham, Richard J. *Jude, 2 Peter.* WBC. Waco, Tex.: Word Books, 1983.

Bauer, Walter. *A Greek-English Lexicon of the New Testament and Other Early Christian Literature.* Tr. and ed. by William F. Arndt and F. Wilbur Gingrich. Rev. and augm. by F. Wilbur Gingrich and Frederick W. Danker. Chicago: University of Chicago Press; Cambridge: Cambridge University Press, 1979.

Baur, Ferdinand Christian. *Vorlesungen über neutestamentliche Theologie* (Lectures on New Testament Theology). Darmstadt: Wissenschaftliche Buchgesellschaft, 1973. (First published 1864).

Beare, Francis W. "The Epistle to the Ephesians: Introduction and Exegesis." *The Interpreter's Bible*, Vol. 10. New York: Abingdon-Cokesbury Press, 1953.

————. *A Commentary on the Epistle to the Philippians.* HNTC. New York: Harper & Brothers, 1959; London: A. & C. Black, 1959; 3d ed. 1973.

————. *The First Epistle of Peter: The Greek Text with Introduction and Notes.* Oxford: Basil Blackwell, 1947; 3d ed. 1970.

————. *The Gospel According to Matthew: A Commentary.* Oxford: Basil Blackwell, 1981; New York: Harper & Row, 1982.

Beasley-Murray, George R. *A Commentary on Mark Thirteen.* London: Macmillan & Co.; New York: St. Martin's Press, 1957.

————. "2 Corinthians." *The Broadman Bible Commentary*, Vol. 11. Nashville: Broadman Press, 1971.

————. *The Book of Revelation.* NCB. London: Oliphants, 1974; Grand Rapids: Wm. B. Eerdmans Publishing Co., 1981.

Beck, Brian E. *Reading the New Testament Today: An Introduction to New Testament Study.* London: Lutterworth Press, 1977; Atlanta: John Knox Press, 1978.

Beker, Johan Christiaan. *Paul the Apostle: The Triumph of God in Life and Thought.* Philadelphia: Fortress Press; Edinburgh: T & T. Clark, 1980.

————. *Paul's Apocalyptic Gospel: The Coming Triumph of God.* Philadelphia: Fortress Press, 1982.

Bernard, John H. *A Critical and Exegetical Commentary on the Gospel According to St. John.* Ed. by A. H. McNeile. ICC. 2 vols. Edinburgh: T. & T. Clark, 1928; New York: Charles Scribner's Sons, 1929. Repr. T. & T. Clark.

————. "The Second Epistle of Paul to the Corinthians." *The Expositor's Greek Testament,* Vol. 3. Edinburgh: T. & T. Clark, 1903. Repr. Grand Rapids: Wm. B. Eerdmans Publishing Co.

Best, Ernest. *A Commentary on the First and Second Epistles to the Thessalonians.* HNTC. New York: Harper & Row; London: A. & C. Black, 1972.

————. *From Text to Sermon: Responsible Use of the New Testament in Preaching.* Atlanta: John Knox Press; Edinburgh: St. Andrew Press, 1978.

————. *1 Peter.* NCB. Grand Rapids: Wm. B. Eerdmans Publishing Co.; London: Marshall, Morgan & Scott, 1982.

Betz, Hans-Dieter. *Galatians: A Commentary on Paul's Letter to the Churches in Galatia.* Hermeneia. Philadelphia: Fortress Press, 1979.

Bicknell, Edward J. *The First and Second Epistles to the Thessalonians.* Westminster Commentaries. London: Methuen & Co., 1932.

Bigg, Charles A. *A Critical and Exegetical Commentary on the Epistles of St. Peter and St. Jude.* ICC. 2d ed. Edinburgh: T. & T. Clark, 1902; New York: Charles Scribner's Sons, 1909. Repr. T. & T. Clark.

Binder, Hermann. *Der Glaube bei Paulus.* Berlin: Evangelische Verlagsanstalt, 1968.

Birdsall, J. Neville. "The New Testament Text." In *The Cambridge History of the Bible*, Vol. 1, ed. by P. R. Ackroyd and C. F. Evans. Cambridge University Press, 1970.

Black, Matthew. *Romans*. NCB. London: Marshall, Morgan & Scott, 1973; Grand Rapids: Wm. B. Eerdmans Publishing Co., 1981.

————, and Rowley, Harold H., eds. *Peake's Commentary on the Bible*. London and New York: Thomas Nelson and Sons, 1962.

Blair, Edward P. *Jesus in the Gospel of Matthew*. New York: Abingdon Press, 1960.

Blass, Friedrich W., and Debrunner, Albert. *A Greek Grammar of the New Testament and Other Early Christian Literature*. Tr. & rev. by Robert W. Funk. Chicago: University of Chicago Press; Cambridge University Press, 1961.

Bligh, John. *Galatians: A Discussion of St. Paul's Epistle*. Middlegreen, Slough, Bucks.: St. Paul Publications, 1969.

Bollier, John. *The Literature of Theology: A Guide for Students and Pastors*. Philadelphia: Westminster Press, 1979.

Bonnard, Pierre. *L'Epître de Saint Paul aux Philippiens*. CNT. Neuchâtel: Delachaux & Niestlé, 1950.

————. *L'Evangile selon Saint Matthieu*. CNT. 2d ed. rev. & augm. Neuchâtel: Delachaux & Niestlé, 1970.

Bornkamm, Günther. *Jesus of Nazareth*. Tr. by Irene and Fraser McLuskey with James M. Robinson. London: Hodder & Stoughton, 1960; New York: Harper & Row, 1961.

————. *Paul*. Tr. by D. M. G. Stalker. New York: Harper & Row, 1971; London: Hodder & Stoughton, 1975.

————; Barth, Gerhard; and Held, Heinz J. *Tradition and Interpretation in Matthew*. Tr. by Percy Scott. Philadelphia: Westminster Press; London: SCM Press, 1963.

Branson, Mark L. *The Reader's Guide to the Best Evangelical Books*. San Francisco: Harper & Row, 1982.

Brauch, Manfred T. "Perspectives on 'God's Righteousness' in Recent German Discussion." In *Paul and Palestinian Judaism: A Comparison of Patterns of Religion*, by E. P.

Sanders. Philadelphia: Fortress Press; London: SCM Press, 1977. Pp. 523–542.

Braun, Herbert. *Jesus of Nazareth: The Man and His Time.* Tr. by Everett R. Kalin. Philadelphia: Fortress Press, 1979.

Bring, Ragnar. *Commentary on Galatians.* Tr. by Eric Wahlstrom. Philadelphia: Muhlenberg Press, 1961.

Bromiley, Geoffrey W., gen. ed. *International Standard Bible Encyclopedia.* Rev. ed. 2 vols. to date. Grand Rapids: Wm. B. Eerdmans Publishing Co., 1979, 1982.

Brown, Colin, ed. *The New International Dictionary of New Testament Theology.* 3 vols. Grand Rapids: Zondervan Publishing House; Exeter: Paternoster Press, 1975–1978.

Brown, Raymond. *Christ Above All: The Message of Hebrews.* Leicester and Downers Grove, Ill.: Inter-Varsity Press, 1982.

Brown, Raymond E. *The Gospel According to John: Introduction, Translation, and Notes.* AB. 2 vols. Garden City, N.Y.: Doubleday & Co., 1966, 1970.

————, gen. ed. *The Jerome Biblical Commentary.* Englewood Cliffs, N.J.: Prentice-Hall; London: Geoffrey Chapman, 1968.

————. *The Birth of the Messiah: A Commentary on the Infancy Narratives in Matthew and Luke.* Garden City, N.Y.: Doubleday & Co.; London: Collier-Macmillan, 1977.

————. *The Community of the Beloved Disciple.* New York: Paulist Press; London: Geoffrey Chapman, 1979.

————. *The Epistles of John: Translated, with Introduction, Notes and Commentary.* AB. Garden City, N.Y.: Doubleday & Co., 1982.

Brown, Schuyler. *Apostasy and Perseverance in the Theology of Luke.* Rome: Biblical Institute Press, 1969.

Bruce, Frederick F. *The Acts of the Apostles: The Greek Text with Introduction and Commentary.* London: Tyndale Press, 1951; Grand Rapids: Wm. B. Eerdmans Publishing Co., 1952.

————. *Commentary on the Book of Acts: The English Text, with Introduction, Exposition, and Notes.* NICNT. Grand Rapids:

Wm. B. Eerdmans Publishing Co.; London: Marshall, Morgan & Scott, 1954.

————. "Colossians." In Simpson, Edmund K., and Bruce, Frederick F. *A Commentary on the Epistles to the Ephesians and the Colossians.* NICNT. Grand Rapids: Wm. B. Eerdmans Publishing Co.; London: Marshall, Morgan & Scott, 1957.

————. *The Epistle to the Ephesians: A Verse-by-Verse Exposition.* London: Pickering & Inglis, 1961; Westwood, N.J.: Fleming H. Revell Co., 1962.

————. *The Epistle of Paul to the Romans: An Introduction and Commentary.* TNTC. Grand Rapids: Wm. B. Eerdmans Publishing Co.; London: Tyndale/Inter-Varsity Press, 1963.

————. *The Epistle to the Hebrews: The English Text with Introduction, Exposition and Notes.* NICNT. Grand Rapids: Wm. B. Eerdmans Publishing Co., 1964; London: Marshall, Morgan & Scott, 1965.

————. *The English Bible: A History of Translations from the Earliest English Versions to the New English Bible.* Rev. ed. London: Lutterworth Press; New York: Oxford University Press, 1970. 3d ed. published by Oxford in 1978 under the title *History of the Bible in English.*

————. *New Testament History.* London: Thomas Nelson & Sons, 1969; Garden City, N.Y.: Doubleday & Co., 1971.

————. *1 and 2 Corinthians.* NCB. London: Oliphants, 1971; Grand Rapids: Wm. B. Eerdmans Publishing Co., 1980.

————. "The History of New Testament Study." In *New Testament Interpretation*, ed. by I. Howard Marshall. Exeter: The Paternoster Press, 1977; Grand Rapids: Wm. B. Eerdmans Publishing Co., 1978. Pp. 21–59.

————. *Paul: Apostle of the Heart Set Free.* Grand Rapids: Wm. B. Eerdmans Publishing Co., 1977. Published by Paternoster Press, Exeter, 1977, under the title *Paul: Apostle of the Free Spirit*; 2d ed. 1980.

————. *The Epistles of John: Introduction, Exposition and Notes.*

Glasgow: Pickering & Inglis, 1978; Grand Rapids: Wm. B. Eerdmans Publishing Co., 1979.

_____. *The Epistle to the Galatians: A Commentary on the Greek Text*. NIGTC. Exeter: Paternoster Press, 1981; Grand Rapids: Wm. B. Eerdmans Publishing Co., 1982.

_____. *An Expanded Paraphrase of the Epistles of Paul*. Exeter: Paternoster Press, 1965. (Published by Wm. B. Eerdmans Publishing Co., Grand Rapids, 1965, under the title *The Letters of Paul: An Expanded Paraphrase*.) Repr. Palm Springs, Calif.: Ronald N. Haynes Publishers, 1981.

_____. *1 & 2 Thessalonians*. WBC. Waco, Tex.: Word Books, 1982.

Buchanan, George W. *To the Hebrews: Translation, Comment, and Conclusions*. AB. Garden City, N.Y.: Doubleday & Co., 1972.

Bultmann, Rudolf. *Theology of the New Testament*. 2 vols. Tr. by Kendrick Grobel. New York: Charles Scribner's Sons, 1951, 1955; London: SCM Press, 1952, 1955.

_____. *The Gospel of John: A Commentary*. Tr. by G. R. Beasley-Murray et al. Oxford: Basil Blackwell; Philadelphia: Westminster Press, 1971.

_____. *The Johannine Epistles: A Commentary on the Johannine Epistles*. Hermeneia. Tr. by R. Philip O'Hara, L. C. McGaughy, and Robert W. Funk. Philadelphia: Fortress Press, 1973.

_____. *Der zweite Brief an die Korinther*. MeyerK. Göttingen: Vandenhoeck & Ruprecht, 1976.

Burnet, Adam W. *The Lord Reigneth*. New York: Charles Scribner's Sons; London: Hodder & Stoughton, 1947.

Burton, Ernest De Witt. *A Critical and Exegetical Commentary on the Epistle to the Galatians*. ICC. Edinburgh: T. & T. Clark, 1920; New York: Charles Scribner's Sons, 1921. Repr. T. & T. Clark.

Buttrick, George A., ed. *The Interpreter's Dictionary of the Bible*. 4 vols. 1962. *Supplementary Volume*, ed. by Keith Crim et al., 1976. Nashville: Abingdon Press.

Caird, George B. *The Gospel of St. Luke.* Pelican New Testament Commentaries. Harmondsworth, Middlesex: Penguin Books, 1964. Published by SCM Press, London, and Westminster Press, Philadelphia, 1978, under the title *Saint Luke.*

————. *A Commentary on the Revelation of St. John the Divine.* HNTC. London: A. & C. Black; New York: Harper & Row, 1966.

————. *Paul's Letters from Prison: Ephesians, Philippians, Colossians, Philemon in the Revised Standard Version: Introduction and Commentary.* New Clarendon Bible. Oxford: University Press, 1976.

Cantinat, Jean. *Les Epîtres de Saint Jacques et de Saint Jude.* SB. Paris: J. Gabalda, 1973.

Carson, Herbert M. *The Epistles of Paul to the Colossians and Philemon: An Introduction and Commentary.* TNTC. Grand Rapids: Wm. B. Eerdmans Publishing Co.; London: Tyndale/Inter-Varsity Press, 1960.

Cartlidge, David R., and Dungan, David L. *Documents for the Study of the Gospels: A Sourcebook for the Comparative Study of the Gospels.* Cleveland: William Collins Publishers; London: William Collins Sons & Co., 1980.

Chaine, Joseph. *L'Epître de Saint Jacques.* EB. Paris: Librairie Lecoffre, 1927.

Charles, Robert H. *A Critical and Exegetical Commentary on the Revelation of Saint John: With Introduction, Notes, and Indices: Also the Greek Text and English Translation.* ICC. 2 vols. Edinburgh: T. & T. Clark; New York: Charles Scribner's Sons, 1920. Repr. T. & T. Clark.

Childs, Brevard S. *Old Testament Books for Pastor and Teacher.* Philadelphia: Westminster Press, 1977.

Coenen, Lothar, gen. ed. *Theologisches Begriffslexikon zum Neuen Testament.* 3 vols. Wuppertal: Theologischer Verlag Rolf Brockhaus, 1967. For E.T., see Brown, Colin.

Cole, Robert Alan. *The Epistle of Paul to the Galatians: An Introduction and Commentary.* TNTC. Grand Rapids: Wm.

B. Eerdmans Publishing Co.; London: Tyndale/Inter-Varsity Press, 1965.

Collange, Jean-François. *The Epistle of Saint Paul to the Philippians.* Tr. by A. W. Heathcote. London: Epworth Press, 1979.

Conybeare, William J., and Howson, J. S. *The Life and Epistles of St. Paul.* Complete and unabridged ed. London: Longman, Brown, 1854 (2 vols.). New York: Charles Scribner's Sons, 1892. Repr. Wm. B. Eerdmans Publishing Co.

Conzelmann, Hans. *The Theology of St. Luke.* Tr. by Geoffrey Buswell. London: Faber & Faber, 1960; New York: Harper & Row, 1961.

_____. *Der Brief an die Kolosser.* NTD. (Part of Vol. 8.) 10th ed. Göttingen: Vandenhoeck & Ruprecht, 1965.

_____. *An Outline of the Theology of the New Testament.* Tr. by John Bowden. New York: Harper & Row; London: SCM Press, 1969.

_____. *Die Apostelgeschichte.* HzNT. 2d ed. Tübingen: J. C. B. Mohr (Paul Siebeck), 1972. E.T. forthcoming in Hermeneia.

_____. *History of Primitive Christianity.* Tr. by John E. Steely. Nashville: Abingdon Press, 1973.

_____. *Jesus: The Classic Article from RGG Expanded and Updated.* Tr. by J. Raymond Lord. Philadelphia: Fortress Press, 1973.

_____. *1 Corinthians: A Commentary on the First Epistle to the Corinthians.* Hermeneia. Tr. by James W. Leitch. Ed. by George W. MacRae. Philadelphia: Fortress Press, 1975.

Cousar, Charles B. *Galatians.* Interpretation. Atlanta: John Knox Press, 1982.

Cranfield, Charles E. B. *The First Epistle of Peter.* London: SCM Press, 1950.

_____. *I & II Peter and Jude: Introduction and Commentary.* Torch Bible Commentaries. London: SCM Press, 1960; New York: Macmillan Co., 1961.

————. *The Gospel According to St. Mark: An Introduction and Commentary.* CGTC. 2d impression with supplementary notes. Cambridge University Press, 1963. Repr. with revisions 1979.

————. *A Critical and Exegetical Commentary on the Epistle to the Romans.* ICC. 6th ed. 2 vols. Edinburgh: T. & T. Clark, 1975, 1979.

Creed, John M. *The Gospel According to St. Luke: The Greek Text with Introduction, Notes and Indices.* London: Macmillan & Co., 1930; New York: St. Martin's Press, 1931.

Crisis for Cranmer and King James. See Schmidt, Michael.

Cross, F. L. *A Synopsis of the First Three Gospels.* 9th ed. Tübingen: J. C. B. Mohr (Paul Siebeck), 1936. (Translation of the Huck-Lietzmann *Synopsis.*)

Cruden, Alexander. *Cruden's Complete Concordance to the Old and New Testaments.* Ed. by A. D. Adams, C. H. Irwin, and S. D. Waters. London: Lutterworth Press; Philadelphia: John C. Winston Co., 1930. Repr. London: Lutterworth Press; Grand Rapids: Zondervan Publishing House.

Cullmann, Oscar. *Christ and Time.* Tr. by Floyd V. Filson. London: SCM Press, 1951; rev. ed. 1962. Philadelphia: Westminster Press, 1950; rev. ed. 1964.

————. *The Christology of the New Testament.* Tr. by Shirley C. Guthrie and Charles A. M. Hall. Philadelphia: Westminster Press; London: SCM Press, 1959; rev. ed. 1963.

————. *The New Testament: An Introduction for the General Reader.* Tr. by Dennis Pardee. Philadelphia: Westminster Press; London: SCM Press, 1968.

Culpepper, R. Alan. *The Johannine School: An Evaluation of the Johannine-School Hypothesis Based on an Investigation of the Nature of Ancient Schools.* Missoula, Mont.: Scholars Press, 1975.

Dahl, Nils A. *The Crucified Messiah, and Other Essays.* Minneapolis: Augsburg Publishing House, 1974.

Dale, Robert W. *The Atonement.* (1875.) London: Congregational Union of England and Wales, 1900.

Dalton, William J. *Christ's Proclamation to the Spirits: A Study of 1 Peter 3:18–4:6.* Analecta Biblica 23. Rome: Pontifical Biblical Institute, 1965.

Danker, Frederick W. *Multipurpose Tools for Bible Study.* 3d ed. St. Louis: Concordia Publishing House, 1970.

Davids, Peter H. *The Epistle of James: A Commentary on the Greek Text.* NIGTC. Grand Rapids: Wm. B. Eerdmans Publishing Co.; Exeter: Paternoster Press, 1982.

Davidson, Andrew B. *The Epistle to the Hebrews: With Introduction and Notes.* Edinburgh: T. & T. Clark, 1982. Repr. Grand Rapids: Zondervan Publishing House, 1950.

Davies, William D. *The Setting of the Sermon on the Mount.* Cambridge University Press, 1976.

————. *Paul and Rabbinic Judaism: Some Rabbinic Elements in Pauline Theology.* London: S.P.C.K., 1948; 4th ed. Philadelphia: Fortress Press, 1980.

Deissmann, Gustav A. *Light from the Ancient East: The New Testament Illustrated by Recently Discovered Texts of the Graeco-Roman World.* 4th ed. Tr. by R. M. Strachan. London and New York: Harper & Brothers, 1927.

Denney, James. "The Epistles to the Thessalonians." *The Expositor's Bible.* London: Hodder & Stoughton, 1894; New York: A. C. Armstrong, 1902. Repr. Wm. B. Eerdmans Publishing Co., 1943.

————. "The Second Epistle to the Corinthians." *The Expositor's Bible.* London: Hodder & Stoughton, 1894; New York: A. C. Armstrong, 1902. Repr. Wm. B. Eerdmans Publishing Co., 1943.

————. *The Death of Christ* (1902). Ed. and rev. by R. V. G. Tasker. London: Tyndale Press, 1951. Repr. Minneapolis: Klock & Klock, 1982.

Dibelius, Martin. *An die Thessalonicher, I, II, An die Philipper.* HzNT. 3d ed. Tübingen: J. C. B. Mohr (Paul Siebeck), 1937.

————. *An die Kolosser, An die Epheser, An Philemon.* HzNT. 3d ed. Ed. by Heinrich Greeven. Tübingen: J. C. B. Mohr (Paul Siebeck), 1953.

————. *Paul.* Ed. and completed by Werner G. Kümmel. Tr. by Frank Clarke. Philadelphia: Westminster Press; London: Longmans, Green & Co., 1953.

————. *The Pastoral Epistles: A Commentary on the Pastoral Epistles.* Hermeneia. Rev. by Hans Conzelmann. Tr. by Philip Buttolph and Adela Yarbro. Philadelphia: Fortress Press, 1972.

————. *James: A Commentary on the Epistle of James.* Hermeneia. Rev. by Heinrich Greeven. Tr. by Michael A. Williams. Philadelphia: Fortress Press, 1976.

Dobschütz, Ernst von. *Die Thessalonicherbriefe.* MeyerK. 7th ed. Göttingen: Vandenhoeck & Ruprecht, 1909. Repr. 1974.

Dodd, Charles H. *The Epistle of Paul to the Romans.* MNTC. London: Hodder & Stoughton; New York: Harper & Brothers, 1932.

————. *The Johannine Epistles.* MNTC. London: Hodder & Stoughton; New York: Harper & Brothers, 1946.

————. *The Interpretation of the Fourth Gospel.* Cambridge University Press, 1953.

————. *Historical Tradition in the Fourth Gospel.* Cambridge University Press, 1963.

Dods, Marcus. "The First Epistle to the Corinthians." *The Expositor's Bible.* 5th ed. New York: A. C. Armstrong; London: Hodder & Stoughton, 1903. Repr. Wm. B. Eerdmans Publishing Co., 1943.

Donfried, Karl P. *1 and 2 Thessalonians.* ICC. Edinburgh: T. & T. Clark, forthcoming.

Douglas, J. D., ed. *The New Bible Dictionary.* 1st ed. London: Tyndale Press; Grand Rapids: Wm. B. Eerdmans Publishing Co., 1962. 2d ed. rev. Leicester: Inter-Varsity Press; Wheaton, Ill.: Tyndale House Publishers, 1982. 2d ed. also published as *The Illustrated Bible Dictionary.* 3 vols. Ed. by N. Hillyer. Leicester: Inter-Varsity Press; Wheaton, Ill.: Tyndale House Publishers, 1980.

Drury, John. *Tradition and Design in Luke's Gospel: A Study in*

Early Christian Historiography. London: Darton, Longman & Todd; Atlanta: John Knox Press, 1976.

Duncan, George S. *The Epistle of Paul to the Galatians*. MNTC. London: Hodder & Stoughton; New York: Harper & Brothers, 1934.

Dunn, James D. G. *Baptism in the Holy Spirit: A Re-examination of the New Testament Teaching on the Gift of the Spirit in Relation to Pentecostalism Today*. London: SCM Press, 1970; Philadelphia: Westminster Press, 1977.

————. *Jesus and the Spirit: A Study of the Religious and Charismatic Experience of Jesus and the First Christians as Reflected in the New Testament*. London: SCM Press, 1975; Philadelphia: Westminster Press, 1979.

————. *Unity and Diversity in the New Testament: An Inquiry Into the Character of Earliest Christianity*. Philadelphia: Westminster Press; London: SCM Press, 1977.

————. *Christology in the Making: A New Testament Inquiry Into the Origins of the Doctrine of the Incarnation*. Philadelphia: Westminster Press; London: SCM Press, 1980.

Easton, Burton Scott. *The Pastoral Epistles: Introduction, Translation, Commentary and Word Studies*. New York: Charles Scribner's Sons; London: SCM Press, 1947.

Eiselen, Frederick C.; Lewis, Edwin; and Downey, David G., eds. *The Abingdon Bible Commentary*. New York: Abingdon Press, 1929. Repr. Abingdon, 1981; also Garden City, N.Y.: Doubleday & Co., 1979.

Elliott, John H. *The Elect and the Holy: An Exegetical Examination of 1 Peter 2:4–10 and the Phrase basileion hierateuma*. Supplement to *Novum Testamentum*. Leiden: E. J. Brill, 1966.

————. "The Rehabilitation of an Exegetical Step-Child: 1 Peter in Recent Research." *Journal of Biblical Literature* 95 (1976): 243–254.

————. *A Home for the Homeless: A Sociological Exegesis of 1 Peter, Its Situation and Strategy*. Philadelphia: Fortress Press, 1981.

Ellis, E. Earle. *The Gospel of Luke.* NCB. London: Oliphants, 1974; Grand Rapids: Wm. B. Eerdmans Publishing Co., 1981.

Ellul, Jacques. *Apocalypse: The Book of Revelation.* Tr. by George W. Schreiner. New York: Seabury Press, 1977.

Farrer, Austin M. *A Rebirth of Images: The Making of St. John's Apocalypse.* Boston: Beacon Press, 1963.

Fee, Gordon D. "The Textual Criticism of the New Testament." In *Biblical Criticism: Historical, Literary, and Textual* by Roland K. Harrison, B. K. Waltke, Donald Guthrie, and Gordon D. Fee. Grand Rapids: Zondervan Publishing House, 1978.

Fenton, John C. *The Gospel of Saint Matthew.* Pelican New Testament Commentaries. Harmondsworth, Middlesex: Penguin Books, 1964. Published by SCM Press, London, and Westminster Press, Philadelphia, 1978, under the title *Saint Matthew.*

Filson, Floyd V. *A Commentary on the Gospel According to St. Matthew.* HNTC. New York: Harper & Row, 1961; London: A. & C. Black, 1960; 2d ed. 1971.

————. *A New Testament History.* Philadelphia: Westminster Press, 1964; London: SCM Press, 1965.

Findlay, George G. *Fellowship in the Life Eternal: An Exposition of the Epistles of St. John.* New York and London: Hodder & Stoughton, 1909.

Findlay, James Alexander. *The Acts of the Apostles.* London: SCM Press, 1934; 2d ed. 1936.

Finegan, Jack. *The Archeology of the New Testament: The Life of Jesus and the Beginning of the Early Church.* Princeton, N.J.. Princeton University Press, 1970.

Fitzmyer, Joseph A. *Pauline Theology: A Brief Sketch.* Englewood Cliffs, N.J.: Prentice-Hall, 1967.

————. *The Gospel According to Luke (I-IX).* AB. Garden City, N.Y.: Doubleday & Co., 1981.

————. *An Introductory Bibliography for the Study of Scripture.* Rev. ed. Rome: Biblical Institute Press, 1981.

Flender, Helmut. *St. Luke: Theologian of Redemptive History*. Tr. by Reginald H. and Ilse Fuller. Philadelphia: Fortress Press; London: S.P.C.K., 1967.

Foakes-Jackson, Frederick J., and Lake, Kirsopp, eds. *The Beginnings of Christianity*. 5 vols. London: Macmillan & Co., 1920–1933. Repr. Grand Rapids: Baker Book House, 1979.

Ford, Josephine Massyngberde. *Revelation: Introduction, Translation, and Commentary*. AB. Garden City, N.Y.: Doubleday & Co., 1975.

Fornberg, Tord. *An Early Church in a Pluralistic Society: A Study of 2 Peter*. Lund: Liber Läromedel/Gleerup, 1977.

Fortna, Robert T. *The Gospel of Signs: A Reconstruction of the Narrative Source Underlying the Fourth Gospel*. SNTS Monograph Series. Cambridge University Press, 1970.

Foulkes, Francis. *The Epistle of Paul to the Ephesians: An Introduction and Commentary*. TNTC. Grand Rapids: Wm. B. Eerdmans Publishing Co.; London: Tyndale/Inter-Varsity Press, 1963.

Frame, James E. *A Critical and Exegetical Commentary on the Epistles of St. Paul to the Thessalonians*. ICC. Edinburgh: T. & T. Clark; New York: Charles Scribner's Sons, 1912. Repr. T. & T. Clark.

France, Richard T. *A Bibliographical Guide to New Testament Research*. 3d ed. Sheffield, England: Journal for the Study of the Old Testament, 1979.

Francis, Fred O., and Meeks, Wayne A., eds. and trs. *Conflict at Colossae: A Problem in the Interpretation of Early Christianity, Illustrated by Selected Modern Studies*. Missoula, Mont.: Scholars Press, 1975.

Franklin, Eric. *Christ the Lord: A Study in the Purpose and Theology of Luke-Acts*. Philadelphia: Westminster Press; London: S.P.C.K., 1975.

Friedrich, Gerhard. *Der Brief an die Philipper*. NTD. (Part of Vol. 8.) 10th ed. Göttingen: Vandenhoeck & Ruprecht, 1962.

Fuller, Reginald H. *A Critical Introduction to the New Testament*. London: Gerald Duckworth & Co., 1966.

――――. "The Pastoral Epistles." In *Ephesians, Colossians, 2 Thessalonians, The Pastoral Epistles*. Proclamation Commentaries. Philadelphia: Fortress Press, 1978.

――――. *The Use of the Bible in Preaching*. Philadelphia: Fortress Press, 1981.

Gadamer, Hans-Georg. *Truth and Method*. 2d ed. Tr. and ed. by G. Barden and J. Cumming. New York: Seabury Press, 1975.

Gasque, W. Ward. *A History of the Criticism of the Acts of the Apostles*. Tübingen: J. C. B. Mohr (Paul Siebeck), 1975; Grand Rapids: Wm. B. Eerdmans Publishing Co., 1976.

Gehman, Henry S., ed. *The New Westminster Dictionary of the Bible*. Philadelphia: Westminster Press, 1970.

Geldenhuys, J. Norval. *Commentary on the Gospel of Luke*. NICNT. Grand Rapids: Wm. B. Eerdmans Publishing Co.; London: Marshall, Morgan & Scott, 1951.

Gentz, William H., ed. *Dictionary of Bible and Religion*. Nashville: Abingdon Press, forthcoming.

Giblin, Charles H. *The Threat to Faith: An Exegetical and Theological Reexamination of 2 Thessalonians 2*. Rome: Pontifical Biblical Institute, 1967.

Gnilka, Joachim. *Der Epheserbrief*. HTKNT. Freiburg: Verlag Herder, 1971.

Godet, Frédéric. *Commentary on the Gospel of St. John: With a Critical Introduction*. 3d ed. Tr. by M. D. Cusin. 3 vols. Edinburgh: T. & T. Clark, 1899–1900. Repr. Grand Rapids: Kregel Publications, 1979.

――――. *Commentary on St. Paul's First Epistle to the Corinthians*. 2 vols. Tr. by A. Cusin. 2 vols. Edinburgh: T. & T. Clark, 1898. Repr. Grand Rapids: Zondervan Publishing House, 1957; Kregel Publications, 1977.

Goodspeed, Edgar J. *The Meaning of Ephesians*. Chicago: University of Chicago Press; London: Cambridge University Press, 1933.

Goppelt, Leonhard. *Apostolic and Post-Apostolic Times.* Tr. by Robert A. Guelich. London: A. & C. Black. Repr. Grand Rapids: Baker Book House, 1977.

————. *Der erste Petrusbrief.* MeyerK. Göttingen: Vandenhoeck & Ruprecht, 1978.

————. *Theology of the New Testament.* Tr. by John E. Alsup. Ed. by Jürgen Roloff. 2 vols. Grand Rapids: Wm. B. Eerdmans Publishing Co., 1981, 1983; London: S.P.C.K., 1982, 1983.

Goulder, Michael D. *Midrash and Lection in Matthew.* Speaker's Lectures in Biblical Studies. London: S.P.C.K., 1974.

Grant, Frederick C., and Rowley, Harold H., eds. *Hastings' Dictionary of the Bible.* 1 vol. New York: Charles Scribner's Sons; Edinburgh: T. & T. Clark, 1963. (Revision of the 1-vol. edition of 1909.)

Grant, Michael. *Saint Paul.* London: George Weidenfeld & Nicolson; New York: Charles Scribner's Sons, 1976.

Grayston, Kenneth. *The Epistles to the Galatians and to the Philippians.* Epworth Preacher's Commentaries. London: Epworth Press, 1957.

————. *The Letters of Paul to the Philippians and to the Thessalonians.* Cambridge Bible Commentary. Cambridge University Press, 1967.

Green, Edward Michael B. *The Second Epistle General of Peter and the General Epistle of Jude: An Introduction and Commentary.* TNTC. Grand Rapids: Wm. B. Eerdmans Publishing Co.; London: Tyndale/Inter-Varsity Press, 1968.

Grier, William J. *The Best Books: A Guide to Christian Literature.* London: Banner of Truth Trust, 1968.

Grollenberg, Lucas H. *Atlas of the Bible.* Tr. and ed. by Joyce M. H. Reid and H. H. Rowley. London: Thomas Nelson & Sons, 1956.

————. *The Penguin Shorter Atlas of the Bible.* Tr. by Mary F. Hedlund. Harmondsworth, Middlesex: Penguin Books, 1978.

Grosheide, Frederik W. *Commentary on the First Epistle to the Corinthians.* NICNT. Grand Rapids: Wm. B. Eerdmans

Publishing Co., 1953; London: Marshall, Morgan & Scott, 1954.

Grundmann, Walter. *Das Evangelium nach Lukas.* THKNT. 2d ed. Berlin: Evangelische Verlagsanstalt, 1961.

———. *Der Brief des Judas und der zweite Brief des Petrus.* THKNT. Berlin: Evangelische Verlagsanstalt, 1974.

Guelich, Robert A. *The Sermon on the Mount: A Foundation for Understanding.* Waco, Tex.: Word Books, 1982.

Gundry, Robert H. *Matthew: A Commentary on His Literary and Theological Art.* Grand Rapids: Wm. B. Eerdmans Publishing Co., 1982.

———. *A Survey of the New Testament.* Exeter: Paternoster Press, 1970; rev. ed. 1979; Grand Rapids: Zondervan Publishing House, 1970; rev. ed. 1982.

Gurnall, William. *The Christian in Complete Armour: A Treatise of the Saints' War Against the Devil* (1655–1662). Repr. London: Banner of Truth Trust, 1964.

Guthrie, Donald. *The Pastoral Epistles: An Introduction and Commentary.* TNTC. Grand Rapids: Wm. B. Eerdmans Publishing Co.; London: Tyndale/Inter-Varsity Press, 1957.

———. *New Testament Introduction.* 3d ed. London: Tyndale Press, 1970; Downers Grove, Ill.: Inter-Varsity Press, 1971.

———. *A Shorter Life of Christ.* Grand Rapids: Zondervan Publishing House, 1970.

———. *New Testament Theology.* Leicester and Downers Grove, Ill.: Inter-Varsity Press, 1981.

———. *Galatians.* NCB. London: Oliphants, 1974; rev. ed., Grand Rapids: Wm. B. Eerdmans Publishing Co., 1981.

———, and Motyer, J. A., gen. eds. *The New Bible Commentary Revised.* 3d ed. Grand Rapids: Wm. B. Eerdmans Publishing Co.; London: Inter-Varsity Press, 1970. (1st ed. was edited by Francis Davidson et al., 1953.)

Haenchen, Ernst. *The Acts of the Apostles: A Commentary.* Tr. by Bernard Noble and Gerald Shinn. Oxford: Basil Blackwell; Philadelphia: Westminster Press, 1971.

Hanson, Anthony T. *The Pastoral Letters: Commentary on the First and Second Letters to Timothy and the Letter to Titus.* Cambridge Bible Commentary. Cambridge University Press, 1966.

———. *Studies in the Pastoral Epistles.* London: S.P.C.K., 1968.

Hanson, Richard P. C. *II Corinthians.* Torch Bible Commentaries. London: SCM Press; New York: Macmillan Co., 1954.

———. *The Acts in the Revised Standard Version: With an Introduction and Commentary.* New Clarendon Bible. Oxford: Clarendon Press, 1967.

Hare, Douglas R. A. *The Theme of Jewish Persecution of Christians in the Gospel According to St. Matthew.* SNTS Monograph Series. Cambridge University Press, 1967.

Harris, Horton. *The Tübingen School.* Oxford: Clarendon Press, 1975.

Harris, Murray J. "2 Corinthians." *The Expositor's Bible Commentary*, Vol. 10. Frank E. Gaebelein, gen. ed. Grand Rapids: Zondervan Publishing House, 1967.

Harrison, Everett F. *A Short Life of Christ.* Grand Rapids: Wm. B. Eerdmans Publishing Co., 1968.

———. *Introduction to the New Testament.* Rev. ed. Grand Rapids: Wm. B. Eerdmans Publishing Co.; Glasgow: Pickering & Inglis, 1971.

———. *Acts: The Expanding Church.* Chicago: Moody Press, 1976.

Harrisville, Roy A. *Romans.* Minneapolis: Augsburg Publishing House, 1980.

Harvey, Anthony E. *Jesus and the Constraints of History.* Philadelphia: Westminster Press; London: S.P.C.K., 1982.

Hasel, Gerhard F. *New Testament Theology: Basic Issues in the Current Debate.* Grand Rapids: Wm. B. Eerdmans Publishing Co., 1978.

Hastings, James, ed. *A Dictionary of the Bible.* 5 vols. New York: Charles Scribner's Sons; Edinburgh: T. & T. Clark, 1898–1904. See also Grant, Frederick C.

Hatch, William H. P. *The Idea of Faith in Christian Literature from the Death of St. Paul to the Close of the Second Century.* Strasbourg: Imprimerie Alsacienne, 1925.

Hawthorne, Gerald F. *Philippians.* WBC. Waco, Tex.: Word Books, 1983.

Hendriksen, William. *More Than Conquerors: An Interpretation of the Book of Revelation.* Grand Rapids: Baker Book House; London: Tyndale Press, 1944. Repr. Baker Book House, 1978.

————. *Exposition of Philippians.* Grand Rapids: Baker Book House, 1962. Repr. (see next entry).

————. *Exposition of Colossians and Philemon.* Grand Rapids: Baker Book House, 1965. Repr. titled *Exposition of Philippians, Colossians, and Philemon,* 1979.

————. *Exposition of the Gospel According to Matthew.* Grand Rapids: Baker Book House, 1973.

————. *Exposition of the Gospel According to Mark.* Grand Rapids: Baker Book House, 1975.

Hengel, Martin. *Judaism and Hellenism: Studies in Their Encounter in Palestine During the Early Hellenistic Period.* Tr. by John Bowden. 2 vols. London: SCM Press, 1974; new ed. 1981; Philadelphia: Fortress Press, 1981.

————. *Acts and the History of Earliest Christianity.* Tr. by John Bowden. London: SCM Press, 1979; Philadelphia: Fortress Press, 1980.

————. *Jews, Greeks and Barbarians: Aspects of the Hellenization of Judaism in the Pre-Christian Period.* Tr. by John Bowden. Philadelphia: Fortress Press; London: SCM Press, 1980.

Héring, Jean. *The First Epistle of Saint Paul to the Corinthians.* Tr. by A. W. Heathcote and P. J. Allcock from 2d ed. in CNT. London: Epworth Press, 1962.

————. *The Second Epistle of Saint Paul to the Corinthians.* Tr. by A. W. Heathcote and P. J. Allcock from 1st ed. in CNT. London: Epworth Press, 1967.

————. *The Epistle to the Hebrews.* Tr. by A. W. Heathcote

and P. J. Allcock from 1st ed. in CNT. London: Epworth Press, 1970.

Hewitt, Thomas. *The Epistle to the Hebrews: An Introduction and Commentary.* TNTC. Grand Rapids: Wm. B. Eerdmans Publishing Co.; London: Tyndale/Inter-Varsity Press, 1960.

Hiebert, David Edmond. *The Thessalonian Epistles: A Call to Readiness: A Commentary.* Chicago: Moody Press, 1971.

―――. *The Epistle of James: Tests of a Living Faith.* Chicago: Moody Press, 1979.

Hill, David. *The Gospel of Matthew.* NCB. London: Oliphants, 1972; Grand Rapids: Wm. B. Eerdmans Publishing Co., 1981.

Hillers, Delbert R. *Covenant: The History of a Biblical Idea.* Baltimore: Johns Hopkins Press, 1969.

Hock, Ronald F. *The Social Context of Paul's Ministry: Tentmaking and Apostleship.* Philadelphia: Fortress Press, 1980.

Hodge, Charles. *A Commentary on the Epistle to the Romans.* Rev. ed. Grand Rapids: L. Kregel, 1886. Repr. Grand Rapids: Wm. B. Eerdmans Publishing Co., 1951; Edinburgh: Banner of Truth Trust, 1972.

―――. *An Exposition of the First Epistle to the Corinthians.* New York: A. C. Armstrong & Son, 1891. Repr. Grand Rapids: Baker Book House, 1980.

Hodgson, Peter C. *The Formation of Historical Theology: A Study of Ferdinand Christian Baur.* New York: Harper & Row, 1966.

Hort, Fenton J. A. *The First Epistle of St. Peter.* London: Macmillan & Co., 1898.

―――. *The Epistle of St. James: The Greek Text with Introduction.* London: Macmillan & Co., 1909.

Horton, Fred L. *The Melchizedek Tradition: A Critical Examination of the Sources to the Fifth Century A.D. and in the Epistle to the Hebrews.* SNTS Monograph Series. Cambridge University Press, 1976.

Hoskyns, Edwyn C. *The Fourth Gospel.* Ed. by Francis Noel Davey. 2d rev. ed. London: Faber & Faber, 1947.

Houlden, James Leslie. *Paul's Letters from Prison: Philippians, Colossians, Philemon, and Ephesians.* Pelican New Testament Commentaries. Harmondsworth, Middlesex: Penguin Books, 1970. London: SCM Press; Philadelphia: Westminster Press, 1977.

————. *A Commentary on the Johannine Epistles.* HNTC. London: A. & C. Black, 1973; New York: Harper & Row, 1974.

————. *The Pastoral Epistles: I and II Timothy, Titus.* Pelican New Testament Commentaries. Harmondsworth, Middlesex: Penguin Books, 1976.

Howard, W. F. *A Grammar of New Testament Greek*, Vol. 2. See Moulton, James H.

Howley, George C. D., gen. ed. *The New Layman's Bible Commentary in One Volume.* Grand Rapids: Zondervan Publishing House, 1979. Published by Pickering & Inglis, Glasgow, 1979, under the title *Bible Commentary for Today.* (The New Testament part was first published in 1969 as *A New Testament Commentary.*)

Hubbard, David A. *The Book of James: Wisdom That Works.* Waco, Tex.: Word Books, 1980.

Huck, Albert, and Greeven, Heinrich. *Synopsis of the First Three Gospels, with the Addition of the Johannine Parallels.* Tübingen: J. C. B. Mohr (Paul Siebeck), 1981; available from Wm. B. Eerdmans Publishing Co., 1982. (A thorough revision of the earlier Huck-Lietzmann *Synopsis.*)

Hughes, Philip E. *Paul's Second Epistle to the Corinthians: The English Text with Introduction, Exposition and Notes.* NICNT. Grand Rapids: Wm. B. Eerdmans Publishing Co.; London: Marshall, Morgan & Scott, 1962.

————. *A Commentary on the Epistle to the Hebrews.* Grand Rapids: Wm. B. Eerdmans Publishing Co., 1977.

Hultgren, Arland J. *Jesus and His Adversaries: The Form and Function of the Conflict Stories in the Synoptic Tradition.* Minneapolis: Augsburg Publishing House, 1979.

Hunt, Ernest W. *Portrait of Paul.* London: A. R. Mowbray & Co., 1968.

Hunter, Archibald M. *The Unity of the New Testament.* London: SCM Press, 1944. Published by Westminster Press, Philadelphia, 1944, under the title *The Message of the New Testament.*

————. *The Epistle to the Romans: Introduction and Commentary.* Torch Bible Commentaries. London: SCM Press; New York: Macmillan Co., 1955.

————. *According to John.* London: SCM Press; Philadelphia: Westminster Press, 1968.

Illustrated Bible Dictionary, The. See Douglas, J. D.

International Standard Bible Encyclopedia. See Bromiley, Geoffrey W.

Interpreter's Dictionary of the Bible, The. See Buttrick, George A.

Jeremias, Joachim. *The Parables of Jesus.* Rev. ed. Tr. by S. H. Hooke. New York: Charles Scribner's Sons; London: SCM Press, 1963.

————. *Die Briefe an Timotheus und Titus.* NTD. (Part of Vol. 9.) Göttingen: Vandenhoeck & Ruprecht, 1963.

————. *New Testament Theology: The Proclamation of Jesus.* (Vol. 1 of his *New Testament Theology.*) Tr. by John Bowden. London: SCM Press; New York: Charles Scribner's Sons, 1971.

Jerome Biblical Commentary, The. See Brown, Raymond E.

Jervell, Jacob. *Luke and the People of God: A New Look at Luke-Acts.* Minneapolis: Augsburg Publishing House, 1972.

Jewett, Robert. *Jesus Against the Rapture: Seven Unexpected Prophecies.* Philadelphia: Westminster Press, 1979.

————. *Letter to Pilgrims: A Commentary on the Epistle to the Hebrews.* New York: Pilgrim Press, 1981.

Johnson, Sherman E. *A Commentary on the Gospel According to St. Mark.* HNTC. London: A. & C. Black, 1960; New York: Harper & Row, 1961.

Judge, Edwin A. *The Social Pattern of Christian Groups in the First Century: Some Prolegomena to the Study of New Testament Ideas of Social Obligation.* London: Tyndale Press, 1960.

Karris, Robert J. *What Are They Saying About Luke and Acts?*
A Theology of the Faithful God. New York: Paulist Press,
1979.

Käsemann, Ernst. *Die Legitimität des Apostels: Eine Untersuch-
ung zu II Korinther 10–13.* Darmstadt: Wissenschaftliche
Buchgesellschaft, 1956.

————. "Ephesians and Acts." In *Studies in Luke-Acts*, ed. by
Leander E. Keck and J. L. Martyn. Nashville: Abingdon
Press, 1966; London: S.P.C.K., 1967. Repr. S.P.C.K.,
1976; Philadelphia: Fortress Press, 1980.

————. *Commentary on Romans.* Tr. and ed. by Geoffrey W.
Bromiley. Grand Rapids: Wm. B. Eerdmans Publishing
Co.; London: SCM Press, 1980.

Kealy, Sean P. *Mark's Gospel: A History of Its Interpretation.*
New York: Paulist Press, 1982.

Keck, Leander E., and Martyn, J. Louis, eds. *Studies in Luke-
Acts.* Nashville: Abingdon Press, 1966; London: S.P.C.K.,
1967. Repr. S.P.C.K., 1976; Philadelphia: Fortress Press,
1980.

————. *The Bible in the Pulpit: The Renewal of Biblical
Preaching.* Nashville: Abingdon Press, 1978.

————. *Paul and His Letters.* Proclamation Commentaries.
Philadelphia: Fortress Press, 1979.

Kee, Howard Clark. *Community of the New Age: Studies in
Mark's Gospel.* Philadelphia: Westminster Press; London:
SCM Press, 1977.

————. *Christian Origins in Sociological Perspective: Methods
and Resources.* Philadelphia: Westminster Press; London:
SCM Press, 1980.

Kelber, Werner H., ed. *The Passion in Mark: Studies on Mark
14–16.* Philadelphia: Fortress Press, 1976.

Kelly, John N. D. *A Commentary on the Pastoral Epistles: I
Timothy, II Timothy, Titus.* HNTC. London: A. & C.
Black, 1963; New York: Harper & Row, 1964.

————. *A Commentary on the Epistles of Peter and of Jude.*
HNTC. New York: Harper & Row; London: A. & C.
Black, 1969.

Kennedy, Harry A. A. "The Epistle to the Philippians." *The Expositor's Greek Testament.* Edinburgh: T. & T. Clark, 1903. Repr. Grand Rapids: Wm. B. Eerdmans Publishing Co.

Kiddle, Martin, and Ross, M. K. *The Revelation of St. John.* MNTC. London: Hodder & Stoughton; New York: Harper & Brothers, 1941.

Kim, Seyoon. *The Origin of Paul's Gospel.* Tübingen: J. C. B. Mohr (Paul Siebeck), 1981; Grand Rapids: Wm. B. Eerdmans Publishing Co., 1982.

Kingsbury, Jack D. *Matthew: Structure, Christology, Kingdom.* Philadelphia: Fortress Press, 1975; London, S.P.C.K., 1976.

Kirby, John C. *Ephesians: Baptism and Pentecost: An Inquiry Into the Structure and Purpose of the Epistle to the Ephesians.* Montreal: McGill University Press; London: S.P.C.K., 1968.

Kittel, Gerhard, and Friedrich, Gerhard. *Theological Dictionary of the New Testament.* 10 vols. Tr. by Geoffrey W. Bromiley. Grand Rapids: Wm. B. Eerdmans Publishing Co., 1964–1976. (E.T. of *Theologisches Wörterbuch zum Neuen Testament.*)

Knox, John. *Philemon Among the Letters of Paul: A New View of Its Place and Importance.* 2d ed. New York: Abingdon Press, 1959; London: William Collins Sons & Co., 1960.

Knox, Wilfred L. *Saint Paul and the Church of the Gentiles.* London: Cambridge University Press; New York: Macmillan Co., 1939.

Koch, Klaus. *The Rediscovery of Apocalyptic.* Tr. by Margaret Kohl. Naperville, Ill.: Alec R. Allenson; London: SCM Press, 1972. Repr. Oxford University Press.

Koester, Helmut. *Introduction to the New Testament.* 2 vols. Hermeneia. Philadelphia: Fortress Press, 1982.

Kopp, Clemens. *The Holy Places of the Gospels.* Tr. by Ronald Walls. New York: Herder & Herder; London: Thomas Nelson & Sons, 1963.

Krodel, Gerhard. *Acts.* Proclamation Commentaries. Philadelphia: Fortress Press, 1981.

Kümmel, Werner G. *The New Testament: The History of the
Investigation of Its Problems.* Tr. by S. McLean Gilmour and
Howard Clark Kee. Nashville: Abingdon Press, 1972;
London: SCM Press, 1973.

———. *The Theology of the New Testament According to Its
Major Witnesses: Jesus, Paul, John.* Tr. by John E. Steely.
Nashville: Abingdon Press, 1973; London: SCM Press,
1974.

———. *Introduction to the New Testament.* Rev. ed. Tr. by
Howard C. Kee. Nashville: Abingdon Press; London: SCM
Press, 1975. Rev. and updated tr. of Kümmel's work,
which is a revision (17th ed.) of Paul Feine and Johannes
Behm, *Einleitung in das Neue Testament.*

Kysar, Robert. *The Fourth Evangelist and His Gospel: An
Examination of Contemporary Scholarship.* Minneapolis:
Augsburg Publishing House, 1975.

Ladd, George E. *A Commentary on the Revelation of John.*
Grand Rapids: Wm. B. Eerdmans Publishing Co., 1972.

———. *A Theology of the New Testament.* Grand Rapids: Wm.
B. Eerdmans Publishing Co., 1974.

Lane, William L. *The Gospel According to Mark: The English
Text with Introduction, Exposition and Notes.* NICNT.
Grand Rapids: Wm. B. Eerdmans Publishing Co.; London:
Marshall, Morgan & Scott, 1974.

Law, Robert. *The Tests of Life: A Study of the First Epistle of St.
John.* Edinburgh: T. & T. Clark, 1914.

Laws, Sophie. *A Commentary on the Epistle of James.* HNTC.
London: A. & C. Black, 1980; San Francisco: Harper &
Row, 1981.

Leaney, Alfred Robert C. *A Commentary on the Gospel According to St. Luke.* HNTC. London: A. & C. Black, 1958; 2d
ed. 1967. Published by Harper & Brothers, New York,
1958, under the title *The Gospel According to St. Luke.*

Leenhardt, Franz J. *The Epistle to the Romans: A Commentary.*
Tr. by Harold Knight. London: Lutterworth Press, 1961.

Liddell, Henry G., and Scott, Robert. *A Greek-English Lexicon.* 9th ed. Rev. and augm. by Henry Stuart Jones et al. Oxford: Clarendon Press, 1940.

Lietzmann, Hans. *An die Römer.* HzNT. 4th ed. Tübingen: J. C. B. Mohr (Paul Siebeck), 1933.

————. *An die Korinther I, II.* HzNT. 5th ed. Rev. by Werner G. Kümmel. Tübingen: J. C. B. Mohr (Paul Siebeck), 1969.

Lightfoot, Joseph B. *The Epistle of St. Paul to the Galatians* (1865). Repr. Grand Rapids: Zondervan Publishing House, 1950.

————. *Saint Paul's Epistle to the Philippians* (1868). London: Macmillan, 1879. Repr. Grand Rapids: Zondervan Publishing House, 1953.

————. *Saint Paul's Epistles to the Colossians and Philemon* (1875). Repr. of 1879 ed. Grand Rapids: Zondervan Publishing House, 1955.

Lightfoot, Robert H. *St. John's Gospel: A Commentary.* Ed. by C. F. Evans. Oxford: Clarendon Press, 1956.

Lincoln, Andrew T. *Ephesians.* WBC. Waco, Tex.: Word Books, forthcoming.

Lindars, Barnabas. *The Gospel of John.* NCB. London: Oliphants, 1972; Grand Rapids: Wm. B. Eerdmans Publishing Co., 1981.

Ljungman, Henrik. *Pistis: A Study of Its Presuppositions and Its Meaning in Pauline Use.* Tr. by W. F. Salisbury. Lund: C. W. K. Gleerup, 1964.

Lock, Walter. *A Critical and Exegetical Commentary on the Pastoral Epistles (I & II Timothy and Titus).* ICC. Edinburgh: T. & T. Clark; New York: Charles Scribner's Sons, 1924. Repr. T. & T. Clark.

Lohmeyer, Ernst. *Der Brief an die Philipper, übersetzt und erklärt.* MeyerK. (Part of Vol. 9.) Rev. by W. Schmauch. Göttingen: Vandenhoeck & Ruprecht, 1953.

Lohse, Eduard. *Colossians-Philemon: A Commentary on the Epistles to the Colossians and Philemon.* Hermeneia. Tr. by

William R. Poehlmann and Robert J. Karris. Philadelphia:
Fortress Press, 1971.
———. *The Formation of the New Testament*. Tr. by M.
Eugene Boring. Nashville: Abingdon Press, 1981.
Luther, Martin. *Lectures on Romans*. Tr. and ed. by Wilhelm
Pauck. Philadelphia: Westminster Press, 1961.
Machen, John Gresham. *New Testament Greek for Beginners*.
New York: Macmillan Co., 1944.
———. *The Virgin Birth of Christ*. 2d ed. 1932. Repr. New
York: Harper & Brothers, 1952.
McHugh, John. *The Mother of Jesus in the New Testament*.
London: Darton, Longman & Todd, 1975.
Mackay, John A. *God's Order: The Ephesian Letter and This
Present Time*. New York: Macmillan Co.; London: James
Nisbet & Co., 1953.
McNeile, Alan H. *The Gospel According to St. Matthew: The
Greek Text with Introduction and Notes*. London: Macmillan
& Co., 1915. Repr. Baker Book House, 1980.
———. *An Introduction to the Study of the New Testament*. 2d
ed. Rev. by C. S. C. Williams. Oxford: Clarendon Press,
1953.
Maddox, Robert. *The Purpose of Luke-Acts*. Göttingen: Van-
denhoeck & Ruprecht; Edinburgh: T. & T. Clark, 1982.
Malherbe, Abraham J. *Social Aspects of Early Christianity*.
Baton Rouge, La.: Louisiana State University Press, 1977.
2d ed. enl. Fortress Press, 1983.
Manson, Thomas W. *The Sayings of Jesus: As Recorded in the
Gospels According to St. Matthew and St. Luke*. London: SCM
Press, 1949. Repr. Grand Rapids: Wm. B. Eerdmans
Publishing Co., 1979.
Manson, William. *The Gospel of Luke*. MNTC. New York:
Harper & Brothers; London: Hodder & Stoughton, 1930.
———. *Jesus the Messiah: The Synoptic Tradition of the Revela-
tion of God in Christ: With Special Reference to Form-
Criticism*. London: Hodder & Stoughton, 1943; Philadel-
phia: Westminster Press, 1946.

————. *The Epistle to the Hebrews: An Historical and Theological Reconsideration.* London: Hodder & Stoughton, 1951.

Manton, Thomas. *An Exposition on the Epistle of James* (1693). Repr. London: Banner of Truth Trust, 1962.

Marsh, John. *The Gospel of St. John.* Pelican New Testament Commentaries. Harmondsworth, Middlesex: Penguin Books, 1968. Published by SCM Press, London, and Westminster Press, Philadelphia, 1978, under the title *Saint John.*

Marshall, Ian Howard. *Luke: Historian and Theologian.* Exeter: Paternoster Press, 1970; Grand Rapids: Zondervan Publishing House, 1971; repr. 1979.

————, ed. *New Testament Interpretation: Essays on Principles and Methods.* Exeter: Paternoster Press, 1977; Grand Rapids: Wm. B. Eerdmans Publishing Co., 1978.

————. *The Gospel of Luke: A Commentary on the Greek Text.* NIGTC. Grand Rapids: Wm. B. Eerdmans Publishing Co.; Exeter: Paternoster Press, 1978.

————. *The Epistles of John.* NICNT. Grand Rapids: Wm. B. Eerdmans Publishing Co.; London: Marshall, Morgan & Scott, 1978.

————. *The Acts of the Apostles: An Introduction and Commentary.* TNTC. Grand Rapids: Wm. B. Eerdmans Publishing Co.; London: Tyndale/Inter-Varsity Press, 1980.

————. *1 and 2 Thessalonians.* NCB. London: Marshall, Morgan & Scott; Grand Rapids: Wm. B. Eerdmans Publishing Co., 1983.

Martin, Ralph P. *The Epistle of Paul to the Philippians: An Introduction and Commentary.* TNTC. London: Tyndale/Inter-Varsity Press, 1959; Grand Rapids: Wm. B. Eerdmans Publishing Co., 1960.

————. *Carmen Christi: Philippians 2:5–11 in Recent Interpretation and in the Setting of Early Christian Worship.* SNTS Monograph Series. Cambridge University Press, 1967. Rev. ed. Grand Rapids: Wm. B. Eerdmans Publishing Co., 1983.

————. "Ephesians." *Broadman Bible Commentary*, Vol. 11. Nashville: Broadman Press, 1971.

————. *Mark: Evangelist and Theologian.* Exeter: Paternoster Press, 1972; Grand Rapids: Zondervan Publishing House, 1973; repr. 1979.

————. *Colossians: The Church's Lord and the Christian's Liberty: An Expository Commentary with a Present-Day Application.* Exeter: Paternoster Press, 1972; Grand Rapids: Zondervan Publishing House, 1973. Repr. Palm Springs, Calif.: Ronald N. Haynes Publishers, forthcoming.

————. *Colossians and Philemon.* NCB. London: Oliphants, 1974. Rev. ed. Grand Rapids: Wm. B. Eerdmans Publishing Co., 1981.

————. *New Testament Foundations: A Guide for Christian Students.* 2 vols. Exeter: Paternoster Press; Grand Rapids: Wm. B. Eerdmans Publishing Co., 1975, 1978.

————. *Philippians.* NCB. London: Oliphants, 1976; Grand Rapids: Wm. B. Eerdmans Publishing Co., 1980.

————. *Reconciliation: A Study of Paul's Theology.* Atlanta: John Knox Press; London: Marshall, Morgan & Scott, 1980.

————. "New Testament Theology: Impasse and Exit." *The Expository Times* 91 (1980): 264–269.

————. *Mark.* Knox Preaching Guides. Atlanta: John Knox Press, 1982.

Martyn, James Louis. *History and Theology in the Fourth Gospel.* 2d ed. rev. and enl. Nashville: Abingdon Press, 1979.

Marxsen, Willi. *Introduction to the New Testament: An Approach to Its Problems.* Tr. by Geoffrey Buswell. Philadelphia: Fortress Press; London: Basil Blackwell, 1968.

————. *Mark the Evangelist: Studies on the Redaction History of the Gospel.* Tr. by James Boyce et al. Nashville: Abingdon Press, 1969.

————. *Der erste Brief an die Thessalonicher.* ZBKNT. Zürich: Theologischer Verlag, 1979.

————. *Der zweite Brief an die Thessalonicher.* ZBKNT. Zürich: Theologischer Verlag, forthcoming.

Masson, Charles. *L'Epître de Saint Paul aux Ephésiens.* CNT. Neuchâtel: Delachaux et Niestlé, 1953.

————. *Les Deux épîtres de Saint Paul aux Thessaloniciens.* CNT. Neuchâtel: Delachaux et Niestlé, 1957.

Mayor, James B. *The Epistle of St. Jude and the Second Epistle of St. Peter: The Greek Text with Introduction, Notes, and Comments.* London: Macmillan & Co.; New York: Macmillan Co., 1907. Repr. Grand Rapids: Baker Book House, 1979.

————. *The Epistle of St. James: The Greek Text with Introduction, Notes, and Comments.* London: Macmillan & Co., 1913. Repr. Grand Rapids: Zondervan Publishing House, 1954; Minneapolis: Klock & Klock, 1977; Baker Book House, 1978.

Mays, James Luther, ed. *Interpreting the Gospels.* Philadelphia: Fortress Press, 1981.

Meeks, Wayne A. *The First Urban Christians: The Social World of the Apostle Paul.* New Haven: Yale University Press, 1983.

Meier, John P. *Matthew.* Wilmington, Del.: Michael Glazier, 1980.

Metzger, Bruce M. *The Text of the New Testament: Its Transmission, Corruption, and Restoration.* 2d ed. Oxford and New York: Oxford University Press, 1968.

————. *A Textual Commentary on the Greek New Testament.* London and New York: United Bible Societies, 1971.

Metzger, Henri. *St. Paul's Journeys in the Greek Orient.* Tr. by S. H. Hooke. London: SCM Press, 1955.

Meyer, Ben F. *The Aims of Jesus.* London: SCM Press, 1979.

Michael, John H. *The Epistle of Paul to the Philippians.* MNTC. London: Hodder & Stoughton, 1928; Garden City, N.Y.: Doubleday & Co., 1929; Harper & Brothers, 1957.

Michaelis, Wilhelm. *Der Brief des Paulus an die Philipper.* THKNT. Leipzig: Deichert, 1935.

Michel, Otto. *Der Brief an die Hebräer, übersetzt und erklärt.* MeyerK. 12th ed. Göttingen: Vandenhoeck & Ruprecht, 1966.

————. "Faith." In *The New International Dictionary of New Testament Theology,* ed. by Colin Brown. Vol. 1. Grand Rapids: Zondervan Publishing House; Exeter: Paternoster Press, 1975. pp. 593–606.

————. *Der Brief an die Römer, übersetzt und erklärt.* MeyerK. 14th ed. Göttingen: Vandenhoeck & Ruprecht, 1978.

Milligan, William. "The Book of Revelation." *The Expositor's Bible.* London: Hodder & Stoughton, 1894; New York: A. C. Armstrong, 1902. Repr. Wm. B. Eerdmans Publishing Co., 1943.

Mitton, Charles Leslie. *The Epistle of James.* London: Marshall, Morgan & Scott; Grand Rapids: Wm. B. Eerdmans Publishing Co., 1966.

————. *Ephesians.* NCB. London: Oliphants, 1976; Grand Rapids: Wm. B. Eerdmans Publishing Co., 1981.

Moffatt, James. *An Introduction to the Literature of the New Testament.* 3d rev. ed. Edinburgh: T. & T. Clark; New York: Charles Scribner's Sons, 1918. Repr. T. & T. Clark.

————. *A Critical and Exegetical Commentary on the Epistle to the Hebrews.* ICC. Edinburgh: T. & T. Clark; New York: Charles Scribner's Sons, 1924. Repr. T. & T. Clark.

————. *A New Translation of the Bible: Containing the Old and New Testaments.* Garden City, N.Y.: Doubleday, Doran & Co., 1928. Rev. ed. New York: Harper & Brothers, 1935.

————. *The General Epistles: James, Peter and Jude.* MNTC. London: Hodder & Stoughton; Garden City, N.Y.: Doubleday, Doran & Co., 1928.

————. *The First Epistle of Paul to the Corinthians.* MNTC. London: Hodder & Stoughton; New York: Harper & Brothers, 1938.

Montefiore, Hugh. *A Commentary on the Epistle to the Hebrews.* HNTC. London: A. & C. Black; New York: Harper & Row, 1964.

Moody, Dale. *The Hope of Glory.* Grand Rapids: Wm. B. Eerdmans Publishing Co., 1964.

Moore, Arthur L. *1 and 2 Thessalonians.* NCB. London: Thomas Nelson & Sons, 1969.

Morgan, Robert, ed. and tr. *The Nature of New Testament Theology: The Contribution of Wilhelm Wrede and Adolf Schlatter.* Naperville, Ill.: Alec R. Allenson; London: SCM Press, 1973.

Morgenthaler, Robert. *Statistik des neutestamentlichen Wortschatzes.* 2d ed. Zürich: Gotthelf Verlag, 1973.

Morris, Leon. *The Apostolic Preaching of the Cross* London: Tyndale Press, 1955; Grand Rapids: Wm. B. Eerdmans Publishing Co., 1956; 3d ed. 1965.

_____. *The Epistles of Paul to the Thessalonians: An Introduction and Commentary.* TNTC. London: Tyndale/Inter-Varsity Press, 1956; Grand Rapids: Wm. B. Eerdmans Publishing Co., 1957.

_____. *The First Epistle of Paul to the Corinthians: An Introduction and Commentary.* TNTC. Grand Rapids: Wm. B. Eerdmans Publishing Co.; London: Tyndale/Inter-Varsity Press, 1958.

_____. *The First and Second Epistles to the Thessalonians: The English Text with Introduction, Exposition, and Notes.* NICNT. Grand Rapids: Wm. B. Eerdmans Publishing Co.; London: Marshall, Morgan & Scott, 1959.

_____. *The Cross in the New Testament.* Grand Rapids: Wm. B. Eerdmans; Exeter: Paternoster Press, 1965.

_____. *The Revelation of St. John: An Introduction and Commentary.* Grand Rapids: Wm. B. Eerdmans Publishing Co. London: Tyndale/Inter-Varsity Press, 1969.

_____. *The Gospel According to John: The English Text with Introduction and Notes.* NICNT. Grand Rapids: Wm. B. Eerdmans Publishing Co., 1970; London: Marshall, Morgan & Scott, 1971.

_____. *Apocalyptic.* 2d ed. Grand Rapids: Wm. B. Eerdmans Publishing Co., 1972.

———. *The Gospel According to St. Luke: An Introduction and Commentary.* TNTC. Grand Rapids: Wm. B. Eerdmans Publishing Co.; London: Tyndale/Inter-Varsity Press, 1974.

Morrison, Clinton. *An Analytical Concordance to the Revised Standard Version of the New Testament.* Philadelphia: Westminster Press, 1979.

Motyer, J. Alec. *The Tests of Faith.* Leicester: Inter-Varsity Press, 1970.

Moule, Charles F. D. *An Idiom-Book of New Testament Greek.* Cambridge University Press, 1953; 2d ed. 1959.

———. *The Epistles of Paul the Apostle to the Colossians and to Philemon.* Cambridge Greek Testament. Cambridge University Press, 1957.

———. *The Birth of the New Testament.* HNTC. 3d rev. ed. London: A. & C. Black, 1981; San Francisco: Harper & Row, 1982.

Moule, Handley C. G. *The Epistle to the Philippians: With Introduction and Notes.* Cambridge Greek Testament. Cambridge University Press, 1897. Repr. Grand Rapids: Baker Book House, 1981.

———. "The Epistle of St. Paul to the Romans." *The Expositor's Bible.* 5th ed. New York: A. C. Armstrong; London: Hodder & Stoughton, 1903. Repr. Wm. B. Eerdmans Publishing Co., 1943.

———. *The Epistle of Paul the Apostle to the Romans: With Introduction and Notes.* Cambridge Bible for Schools and Colleges. Cambridge University Press, 1908.

———. *The Cross and the Spirit.* Glasgow: Pickering & Inglis, n.d.

Moulton, James H., and W. F. Howard. *A Grammar of New Testament Greek.* Edinburgh: T. & T. Clark. Vol. I, *Prolegomena,* by Moulton, 3d ed., 1908; Vol II, *Accidence and Word-Formation,* by Moulton and Howard, 1929; Vol. III, *Syntax,* by Nigel Turner, 1963; Vol. IV, *Style,* by Turner, 1976.

Mounce, Robert H. *The Book of Revelation.* NICNT. Grand Rapids: Wm. B. Eerdmans Publishing Co., 1977; London: Marshall, Morgan & Scott, 1978.

Müller, Jacobus J. *The Epistles of Paul to the Philippians and to Philemon.* NICNT. Grand Rapids: Wm. B. Eerdmans Publishing Co.; London: Marshall, Morgan & Scott, 1955.

Munck, Johannes. *The Acts of the Apostles: Introduction, Translation, and Notes.* AB. Rev. by W. F. Albright and C. S. Mann. Garden City, N.Y.: Doubleday & Co., 1967.

_____. *Christ and Israel: An Interpretation of Romans 9–11.* Philadelphia: Fortress Press, 1967.

Murphy-O'Connor, Jerome. *1 Corinthians.* Wilmington, Del.: Michael Glazier, 1980.

Murray, Andrew. *The Holiest of All: An Exposition of the Epistle to the Hebrews.* New York: Fleming H. Revell, 1908. Repr. New York: Fleming H. Revell; London: Oliphants, 1960.

Murray, John. *The Epistle to the Romans: The English Text with Introduction, Exposition, and Notes.* NICNT. 2 vols. Grand Rapids: Wm. B. Eerdmans Publishing Co., 1959–66; London: Marshall, Morgan & Scott, 1960–1967.

Mussner, Franz. *Der Jacobusbrief.* HTKNT. Freiburg: Verlag Herder, 1964.

Neil, William. *The Epistle of Paul to the Thessalonians.* MNTC. London: Hodder & Stoughton; New York: Harper & Brothers, 1950.

_____. *The Letter of Paul to the Galatians.* Cambridge Bible Commentary. Cambridge University Press, 1967.

_____. *The Acts of the Apostles.* NCB. London: Oliphants, 1973; rev. ed. Grand Rapids: Wm. B. Eerdmans Publishing Co., 1981.

Neill, Stephen C. *The Interpretation of the New Testament 1861–1961.* London and New York: Oxford University Press, 1964.

Nestle, Erwin, and Aland, Kurt, eds. *Novum Testamentum Graece.* 26th ed. Stuttgart: Deutsche Bibelstiftung, 1979.

New Bible Dictionary, The. See Douglas, J. D.

New International Dictionary of New Testament Theology, The. See Brown, Colin.

New Westminster Dictionary of the Bible, The. See Gehman, Henry S.

Nickelsburg, George W. E. *Jewish Literature Between the Bible and the Mishnah: A Historical and Literary Introduction.* Philadelphia: Fortress Press, 1981.

Nineham, Dennis E. *The Gospel of Saint Mark.* Pelican New Testament Commentaries. Harmondsworth, Middlesex: Penguin Books, 1963. Published by SCM Press, London, and Westminster Press, Philadelphia, 1977, under the title *Saint Mark.*

Nock, Arthur D. *St. Paul.* New York: Harper & Brothers, 1938; Oxford: Clarendon Press, 1946.

Nunn, Henry P. V., and Wenham, John. *The Elements of New Testament Greek.* Cambridge University Press, 1965.

Nygren, Anders. *Commentary on Romans.* Tr. by Carl C. Rasmussen. Philadelphia: Muhlenberg Press, 1949; London: SCM Press, 1952.

O'Brien, Peter T. *Colossians, Philemon.* WBC. Waco, Tex.: Word Books, 1982.

O'Neill, John C. *The Theology of Acts in Its Historical Setting.* 2d rev. ed. London: S.P.C.K., 1970.

Painter, John. *John: Witness and Theologian.* London: S.P.C.K., 1975; rev. ed. 1979.

Palmer, Earl F. *Salvation by Surprise: Studies in the Book of Romans.* Waco, Tex.: Word Books, 1975.

Parry, R. St. John. *The First Epistle of Paul the Apostle to the Corinthians.* Cambridge Greek Testament. Cambridge University Press, 1937.

Patzia, Arthur G. "The Deutero-Pauline Hypothesis: An Attempt at Clarification." *Evangelical Quarterly* 52 (1980):27–42.

Perrin, Norman. *The New Testament, An Introduction: Proclamation and Parenesis, Myth and History.* New York: Harcourt Brace Jovanovich, 1974. 2d ed., rev. by Dennis C. Duling, 1982.

Pfeiffer, Charles F., and Harrison, Everett F., eds. *The Wycliffe Bible Commentary.* Chicago: Moody Press, 1962; London: Oliphants, 1963.

Plummer, Alfred. *A Critical and Exegetical Commentary on the Gospel According to St. Luke.* ICC. 5th ed. Edinburgh: T. & T. Clark, 1922; New York: Charles Scribner's Sons, 1910. Repr. T. & T. Clark.

Rackham, Richard B. *The Acts of the Apostles: An Exposition.* 9th ed. London: Methuen & Co., 1922.

Rahlfs, Alfred, ed. *Septuaginta.* Stuttgart: Württembergische Bibelanstalt, 1979.

Ramsay, William M. *The Church in the Roman Empire Before A.D. 170.* London: Hodder & Stoughton, 1893.

Rawlinson, Alfred E. J. *St. Mark: With Introduction, Commentary, and Additional Notes.* Westminster Commentaries. 7th ed. London: Methuen & Co., 1949.

Reicke, Bo. *The Epistles of James, Peter, and Jude: Introduction, Translation, and Notes.* AB. Garden City, N.Y.: Doubleday & Co., 1964.

————. *The Gospel of Luke.* Tr. by Ross Mackenzie. Richmond: John Knox Press, 1964.

————. *The New Testament Era: The World of the Bible from 500 B.C. to A.D. 100.* Tr. by David E. Green. Philadelphia: Fortress Press, 1968; London: A. & C. Black, 1969.

Rendall, Gerald H. *The Epistle of St. James and Judaic Christianity.* Cambridge University Press, 1927.

Reumann, John H. P. *Righteousness in the New Testament: Justification in the Lutheran-Catholic Dialogue.* Philadelphia: Fortress Press, 1982.

Richardson, Alan, ed. *A Theological Word Book of the Bible.* London: SCM Press, 1950; New York: Macmillan Co., 1951.

————. *An Introduction to the Theology of the New Testament.* New York: Harper & Brothers; London: SCM Press, 1958.

Ridderbos, Herman N. *The Epistle of Paul to the Churches of Galatia.* NICNT. Tr. by H. Zylstra. Grand Rapids: Wm. B. Eerdmans Publishing Co., 1953. Published by Marshall,

Morgan & Scott, 1953, under the title *Epistle to the Galatians*.

————. *Paul: An Outline of His Theology.* Tr. by John R. DeWitt. Grand Rapids: Wm. B. Eerdmans Publishing Co., 1975; London: S.P.C.K., 1977.

Rigaux, Béda. *Saint Paul: Les Epîtres aux Thessaloniciens.* EB. Paris: Lecoffre, 1956.

Robertson, Archibald, and Plummer, Alfred. *A Critical and Exegetical Commentary on the First Epistle of St. Paul to the Corinthians.* ICC. 2d ed. Edinburgh: T. & T. Clark, 1914; New York: Charles Scribner's Sons, 1925. Repr. T. & T. Clark.

Robertson, Archibald T. *A Grammar of the Greek New Testament in the Light of Historical Research.* 4th ed. Nashville: Broadman Press, 1934.

Robinson, James M. *The Problem of History in Mark.* London: SCM Press, 1957. Rev. ed., titled *The Problem of History in Mark and Other Marcan Studies,* published by Fortress Press, Philadelphia, 1983.

Robinson, John A. T. *Wrestling with Romans.* Philadelphia: Westminster Press; London: SCM Press, 1979.

Robinson, Joseph Armitage. *St. Paul's Epistle to the Ephesians: A Revised Text and Translation with Exposition and Notes.* 2d ed. London: Macmillan & Co., 1928.

Robinson, Theodore H. *The Epistle to the Hebrews.* MNTC. New York: Harper & Brothers; London: Hodder & Stoughton, 1933.

Ropes, John H. *A Critical and Exegetical Commentary on the Epistle of St. James.* ICC. Edinburgh: T. & T. Clark; New York: Charles Scribner's Sons, 1916. Repr. T. & T. Clark.

Rowland, Christopher. *The Open Heaven: A Study of Apocalyptic in Judaism and Early Christianity.* New York: Crossroad Publishing Co.; London: S.P.C.K., 1982.

Ruef, John S. *Paul's First Letter to Corinth.* Pelican New Testament Commentaries. Harmondsworth, Middlesex: Penguin Books, 1971. London: SCM Press; Philadelphia: Westminster Press, 1977.

Russell, David S. *The Method and Message of Jewish Apocalyptic: 200 B.C.–A.D. 100.* Philadelphia: Westminster Press; London: SCM Press, 1964.

Sanday, William, and Headlam, Arthur C. *A Critical and Exegetical Commentary on the Epistle to the Romans.* ICC. 5th ed. Edinburgh: T. & T. Clark, 1902; 12th ed. New York: Charles Scribner's Sons, 1910. Repr. T. & T. Clark.

Sanders, Ed P. *Paul and Palestinian Judaism: A Comparison of Patterns of Religion.* Philadelphia: Fortress Press; London: SCM Press, 1977.

Sanders, Joseph N. *A Commentary on the Gospel According to St. John.* HNTC. Ed. by B. A. Mastin. New York: Harper & Row; London: A. & C. Black, 1968.

Schelkle, Karl H. *Die Petrusbriefe, Der Judasbrief.* HTKNT. Freiburg: Verlag Herder, 1961.

Schlatter, Adolf von. *Die Theologie des Neuen Testaments.* 2 vols. Stuttgart: Calwer Verlag der Vereinsbuchhandlung, 1909–1910.

Schlier, Heinrich. *Der Brief an die Epheser. Ein Kommentar.* Düsseldorf: Patmos-Verlag, 1963.

Schmid, Josef. *The Gospel According to Mark.* The Regensburg New Testament. Tr. by Kevin Condon. Cork, Ireland: Mercier Press, 1968; New York: Alba House, 1969.

Schmidt, Michael, gen. ed. *Crisis for Cranmer and King James.* (*PN Review* 13, Vol. 6, No. 5.) Manchester: Carcanet Press, 1979.

Schmithals, Walter. *Gnosticism in Corinth: An Investigation of the Letters to the Corinthians.* Tr. by John E. Steely. Nashville: Abingdon Press, 1971.

———. *Paul and the Gnostics.* Tr. by John E. Steely. Nashville: Abingdon Press, 1972.

Schnackenburg, Rudolf. *The Gospel According to St. John.* Tr. by C. Hastings. 3 vols. (1968, 1979, 1982). New York: Crossroad Publishing Co.; London: Burns & Oates.

Scholer, David M. *A Basic Bibliographic Guide for New Testament Exegesis.* 2d ed. Grand Rapids: Wm. B. Eerdmans Publishing Co., 1973.

Schürmann, Heinz. *Das Lukasevangelium*. HTKNT. Freiburg: Verlag Herder, 1969.

Schweizer, Eduard. *The Good News According to Mark*. Tr. by Donald Madvig. John Knox Press, 1970.

———. *Jesus*. Tr. by David E. Green. London: SCM Press; Atlanta: John Knox Press, 1971.

———. *The Good News According to Matthew*. Tr. by David E. Green. Atlanta: John Knox Press, 1975.

———. *Luke: A Challenge to Present Theology*. Atlanta: John Knox Press, 1982.

———. *The Letter to the Colossians: A Commentary*. Tr. by Andrew Chester. Minneapolis: Augsburg Publishing House; London: S.P.C.K., 1982.

Scott, Charles A. Anderson. *Christianity According to St. Paul*. Cambridge University Press, 1932.

———. *St. Paul: The Man and the Teacher*. Cambridge: Cambridge University Press; New York: Macmillan Co., 1936.

Scott, Ernest F. *The Epistles of Paul to the Colossians, to Philemon and to the Ephesians*. MNTC. New York: Harper & Brothers; London: Hodder & Stoughton, 1930.

———. *Paul's Epistle to the Romans*. London: SCM Press, 1947. Repr. Westport, Conn.: Greenwood Press, 1979.

Selwyn, Edward G. *The First Epistle of St. Peter: The Greek Text, with Introduction, Notes, and Essays*. London: Macmillan & Co., 1946; New York: St. Martin's Press, 1952. Repr. Grand Rapids: Baker Book House, 1981.

Shepherd, Massey H., Jr. *The Psalms in Christian Worship: A Practical Guide*. Minneapolis: Augsburg Publishing House, 1976.

Sherwin-White, Adrian N. *Roman Society and Roman Law in the New Testament*. Oxford: Clarendon Press, 1963.

Sidebottom, E. M. *James, Jude, 2 Peter: Based on the Revised Standard Version*. NCB. Grand Rapids: Wm. B. Eerdmans Publishing Co.; London: Marshall, Morgan & Scott, 1982.

Simpson, Edmund K. *The Pastoral Epistles: The Greek Text, with Introduction and Commentary*. Grand Rapids: Wm. B.

Eerdmans Publishing Co.; London: Tyndale/Inter-Varsity Press, 1954.

―――. "Ephesians." In Simpson, Edmund K., and Bruce, Frederick F. *A Commentary on the Epistles to the Ephesians and the Colossians.* NICNT. Grand Rapids: Wm. B. Eerdmans Publishing Co.; London: Marshall, Morgan & Scott, 1957.

Smalley, Stephen S. *John, Evangelist and Interpreter.* Exeter: Paternoster Press, 1978.

Smith, Dwight Moody. *Interpreting the Gospels for Preaching.* Philadelphia: Fortress Press, 1980.

Smith, George Adam. *The Historical Geography of the Holy Land: Especially in Relation to the History of Israel and of the Early Church.* 25th ed. London: Hodder & Stoughton; New York: Harper & Brothers, 1931. Repr. London: William Collins Sons & Co., Fontana Books, 1966; Magnolia, Mass.: Peter Smith.

Smith, Wilbur M. "Bible Dictionaries and Encyclopedias." *International Standard Bible Encyclopedia.* Rev. ed. Ed. by Geoffrey W. Bromiley. Vol. 1. Wm. B. Eerdmans Publishing Co., 1979. Pp. 492–498.

Spicq, Ceslaus. *L'Epître aux Hébreux.* EB. 2 vols. Paris: J. Gabalda, 1952–1953.

―――. *Les Epîtres de Saint Pierre.* SB. Paris: J. Gabalda, Librairie Lecoffre, 1966.

―――. *Saint Paul: Les Epîtres Pastorales.* EB. 4th rev. ed. Paris: J. Gabalda, 1969.

Stauffer, Ethelbert. *New Testament Theology.* Tr. by John Marsh. London: SCM Press, 1955; New York: Macmillan Co., 1956.

Stendahl, Krister. *The School of St. Matthew: And Its Use of the Old Testament.* Uppsala: C. W. K. Gleerup, 1954; 2d ed., 1968. Repr. Philadelphia: Fortress Press, 1968.

Stewart, James S. *A Man in Christ: The Vital Elements of St. Paul's Religion.* London: Hodder & Stoughton; New York: Harper & Brothers, 1935. Repr. Grand Rapids: Baker Book House, 1975.

Stibbs, Alan M. *The First Epistle General of Peter: A Commentary*. TNTC. Grand Rapids: Wm. B. Eerdmans Publishing Co.; London: Tyndale/Inter-Varsity Press, 1959.

Stott, John R. W. *The Epistles of John: An Introduction and Commentary*. TNTC. Grand Rapids: Wm. B. Eerdmans Publishing Co.; London: Tyndale/Inter-Varsity Press, 1964.

————. *Men Made New: An Exposition of Romans 5–8*. London and Downers Grove, Ill.: Inter-Varsity Press, 1966.

Strachan, Robert H. *The Fourth Gospel: Its Significance and Environment*. London: SCM Press, 1917. 3d rev. ed. London: SCM Press; New York: Macmillan Co., 1941.

————. *The Second Epistle of Paul to the Corinthians*. MNTC. London: Hodder & Stoughton, 1935; New York: Harper & Brothers, 1936.

Strong, James. *The Exhaustive Concordance of the Bible*. New York: Hunt & Eaton, 1890. Repr. New York: Thomas Nelson & Sons.

Stuhlmacher, Peter. *Historical Criticism and Theological Interpretation of Scripture: Toward a Hermeneutics of Consent*. Tr. by Roy A. Harrisville. Philadelphia: Fortress Press, 1977; London: S.P.C.K., 1979.

Swanson, Reuben J. *The Horizontal Line Synopsis of the Gospels*. Dillsboro: Western North Carolina Press, 1975.

————. *The Horizontal Line Synopsis of the Gospels, Greek Edition*. Vol. 1. *The Gospel of Matthew*. Dillsboro: Western North Carolina Press, 1982.

Sweet, John P. M. *Revelation*. Pelican New Testament Commentaries. London: SCM Press; Philadelphia: Westminster Press, 1979.

Swete, Henry B., ed. *The Old Testament in Greek According to the Septuagint*. 3 vols. Cambridge University Press, 1895–1899.

————. *The Apocalypse of St. John: The Greek Text with Introduction, Notes, and Indices*. 3d ed. London: Macmillan & Co., 1917. Repr. Grand Rapids: Kregel Publications, 1978, under the title *Commentary on Revelation*.

Synge, Francis C. *Philippians and Colossians: Introduction and Commentary.* Torch Bible Commentaries. London: SCM Press; New York: Macmillan & Co., 1951.

Tasker, Randolph V. G. *The General Epistle of James: An Introduction and Commentary.* TNTC. London: Tyndale/ Inter-Varsity Press, 1956; Grand Rapids: Wm. B. Eerdmans Publishing Co., 1957.

————. *The Second Epistle of Paul to the Corinthians: An Introduction and Commentary.* TNTC. Grand Rapids: Wm. B. Eerdmans Publishing Co.; London: Tyndale/Inter-Varsity Press, 1958.

————. *The Gospel According to St. John: An Introduction and Commentary.* TNTC. Grand Rapids: Wm. B. Eerdmans Publishing Co.; London: Tyndale/Inter-Varsity Press, 1960.

Taylor, Vincent. *The Gospel According to St. Mark: The Greek Text with Introduction, Notes and Indexes.* London: Macmillan & Co.; New York: St. Martin's Press, 1952. 2d ed. London: Macmillan & Co., 1966; Grand Rapids: Baker Book House, 1981.

Temple, William. *Readings in St. John's Gospel.* 2 vols. London: Macmillan & Co., 1939–1940. Repr. New York: St. Martin's Press, 1959.

Tenney, Merrill C. *John: The Gospel of Belief: An Analytic Study of the Text.* NICNT. Grand Rapids: Wm. B. Eerdmans Publishing Co.; London: Marshall, Morgan & Scott, 1948.

————, gen. ed. *The Zondervan Pictorial Encyclopedia of the Bible.* 5 vols. Grand Rapids: Zondervan Publishing House, 1975.

Theissen, Gerd. *Sociology of Early Palestinian Christianity.* Tr. by John Bowden. Philadelphia: Fortress Press, 1978. Published by SCM Press, London, 1978, under the title *The First Followers of Jesus: A Sociological Analysis of the Earliest Christianity.*

————. *The Social Setting of Pauline Christianity: Essays on*

Corinth. Ed. & tr. by John H. Schütz. Philadelphia: Fortress Press; London: SCM Press, 1982.

Theologisches Begriffslexikon zum Neuen Testament. See Coenen, Lothar.

Thiselton, Anthony C. "New Testament Commentary Survey." *The Theological Students' Fellowship Bulletin* 58 (1970):9–18. Revised by Donald A. Carson and issued separately in 1977.

————. "Semantics" and "The New Hermeneutic." *New Testament Interpretation.* Ed. by I. Howard Marshall. Exeter: Paternoster Press, 1977; Grand Rapids: Wm. B. Eerdmans Publishing Co., 1978.

————. *The Two Horizons.* Exeter: Paternoster Press, 1979; Grand Rapids: Wm. B. Eerdmans Publishing Co., 1980.

Thompson, George H. P. *The Letters of Paul to the Ephesians, to the Colossians and to Philemon.* Cambridge Bible Commentary. Cambridge University Press, 1967.

Thompson, John A. *The Bible and Archaeology.* 2d rev. ed. Grand Rapids: Wm. B. Eerdmans Publishing Co., 1972; Exeter: Paternoster Press, 1973.

Thrall, Margaret E. *The First and Second Letters of Paul to the Corinthians.* Cambridge Bible Commentary. Cambridge University Press, 1965.

Throckmorton, Burton H. *Gospel Parallels: A Synopsis of the First Three Gospels.* 2d rev. ed. New York: Thomas Nelson & Sons, 1957. (Revised Standard Version.)

Trocmé, Etienne. *The Formation of the Gospel According to Mark.* Tr. by Pamela Gaughan. Philadelphia: Westminster Press, 1975.

Trotti, John B., ed. *Aids to a Theological Library.* Missoula, Mont.: Scholars Press, 1977.

Turner, Nigel. *A Grammar of New Testament Greek,* Vols. 3, 4. See Moulton, James H.

————. *Grammatical Insights Into the New Testament.* Edinburgh: T. & T. Clark, 1966.

————. *Christian Words.* Edinburgh: T. & T. Clark, 1980; New York: Thomas Nelson & Sons, 1982.

Vincent, Marvin R. *A Critical and Exegetical Commentary on the Epistles to the Philippians and to Philemon.* ICC. Edinburgh: T. & T. Clark, 1897; New York: Charles Scribner's Sons, 1903. Repr. T. & T. Clark.

Wagner, Günter, ed. *An Exegetical Bibliography of the New Testament.* Rüschlikon-Zürich: Baptist Theological Seminary, 1973–. Vol. 1. *Matthew and Mark.* Macon, Ga.: Mercer University Press, 1982.

Wand, John W. C. *The General Epistles of St. Peter and St. Jude.* Westminster Commentaries. London: Methuen & Co., 1934.

Ward, Ronald A. *Hidden Meaning in the New Testament: New Light from the Old Greek.* London: Marshall, Morgan & Scott; Westwood, N.J.: Fleming H. Revell Co., 1969.

_____. *Commentary on 1 and 2 Thessalonians.* Waco, Tex.: Word Books, 1973.

Weber, Hans-Ruedi. *The Cross: Tradition and Interpretation.* Tr. by Elke Jessett. Grand Rapids: Wm. B. Eerdmans Publishing Co.; London: S.P.C.K., 1979.

Wesley, John. *Explanatory Notes Upon the New Testament* (1755). London: Epworth Press, 1948. Repr. of 1950 ed. Geneva, Ala.: Allenson-Breckinridge Books.

Westcott, Brooke F. *The Gospel According to St. John: The Authorized Version, with Introduction and Notes.* London: J. Murray, 1881. Repr. Grand Rapids: Wm. B. Eerdmans Publishing Co., 1950; London: James Clarke & Co., 1958.

_____. *The Gospel According to St. John: The Greek Text with Introduction and Notes.* London: J. Murray, 1908. Repr., 2 vols. in 1. Grand Rapids: Wm. B. Eerdmans Publishing Co., 1954; Baker Book House, 1980.

_____. *The Epistles of St. John: The Greek Text with Notes* (1883). New ed. with Introduction by F. F. Bruce. Abingdon, Berks.: Marcham Manor Press, 1966.

_____. *The Epistle to the Hebrews: The Greek Text with Notes and Essays* (1889). 3d ed. London: Macmillan & Co., 1920. Repr. Grand Rapids: Wm. B. Eerdmans Publishing Co., 1950.

Whiteley, Denys E. H. *Thessalonians in the Revised Standard Version: With Introduction and Commentary.* New Clarendon Bible. London: Oxford University Press, 1969.

Wikenhauser, Alfred. *New Testament Introduction.* Tr. by Joseph Cunningham. New York: Herder & Herder, 1958.

Wilckens, Ulrich. *Der Brief an die Römer.* EKK. Zürich: Benziger Verlag; Neukirchen-Vluyn, Neukirchener Verlag, 1978.

Wilcock, Michael. *I Saw Heaven Opened: The Message of Revelation.* Leicester and Downers Grove, Ill.: Inter-Varsity Press, 1975.

Wilkinson, John D. *Jerusalem as Jesus Knew It: Archaeology as Evidence.* London: Thames & Hudson, 1978.

Williams, Charles S. C. *A Commentary on the Acts of the Apostles.* HNTC. New York: Harper & Brothers; London: A. & C. Black, 1957; 2d ed. 1964.

Williamson, Lamar. *Mark.* Interpretation. Atlanta: John Knox Press, 1983.

Williamson, Ronald. *Philo and the Epistle to the Hebrews.* Supplement to *Novum Testamentum.* Leiden: E. J. Brill, 1970.

Wilson, Geoffrey B. *A Digest of Reformed Comment.* Edinburgh: Banner of Truth Trust, 1969–1982. Covers all the Pauline epistles except Philippians, I and II Timothy, and Titus. Includes Hebrews.

Wilson, Stephen G. *The Gentiles and the Gentile Mission in Luke-Acts.* SNTS Monograph Series. Cambridge University Press, 1973.

————. *Luke and the Pastoral Epistles.* London: S.P.C.K., 1979.

Windisch, Hans, and Preisker, Herbert. *Die katholischen Briefe.* HzNT. 3d ed. Tübingen: J. C. B. Mohr (Paul Siebeck), 1951.

Wink, Walter P. *The Bible in Human Transformation: Towards a New Paradigm for Biblical Study.* Philadelphia: Fortress Press, 1973.

Wright, George Ernest, and Filson, Floyd V. *The Westminster Historical Atlas to the Bible.* Rev. ed. Philadelphia: Westminster Press, 1956.

Wuest, Kenneth S. *Expanded Translation of the Greek New Testament.* Grand Rapids: Wm. B. Eerdmans Publishing Co., 1956–1959; London: Pickering & Inglis, 1957–1959. Published in 1 vol. by Eerdmans and by Pickering & Inglis, 1961, under the title *The New Testament: An Expanded Translation.*

Yoder, Perry B., and Yoder, Elizabeth. *Toward Understanding the Bible.* Newton, Kans.: Faith & Life Press, 1978.

Young, Robert. *Analytical Concordance to the Bible.* 6th ed. Edinburgh: George Adam Young & Co., n.d.; Grand Rapids: Wm. B. Eerdmans Publishing Co., 1955.

Ziesler, John A. *The Meaning of Righteousness in Paul: A Linguistic and Theological Enquiry.* SNTS Monograph Series. Cambridge University Press, 1972.

Zondervan Pictorial Encyclopedia of the Bible, The. See Tenney, Merrill C.

Appendix

Those who have noted titles which they particularly wish to have—especially when the books are out of print—may be glad to have a list of used book dealers and outlets that specialize in biblical volumes. In addition to the information that Childs gives, let me note the following items.

1. *The United States*

John Wipf, The Archives, 1387 E. Washington, Pasadena, CA 91104.

Baker Book House, 1019 Wealthy St., Grand Rapids, MI 49506.

Kregel's Bookstore, 525 Eastern Ave., Grand Rapids, MI 49503.

Noah's Ark Book Attic, Stony Point, Rt. 2, Greenwood, SC 29646.

Richard Owen Roberts, 205 E. Kehoe Blvd., Wheaton, IL 60187.

Stevens Book Shop, 245 E. Roosevelt, Wake Forest, NC 27587.

2. *Great Britain*

B. H. Blackwell, Ltd., 50 Broad Street, Oxford, England OX1 3BQ.

Holleyman and Son, 59 Carlisle Road, Hove, Sussex, England BN3 4FQ.

Howes Bookshop, 3 Trinity St., Hastings, Sussex, England TN34 1HQ.

Nelson's Bookroom, Lydbury, North Shropshire, England SY7 8AS.

James Thin, 53–59 South Bridge, Edinburgh, Scotland.

W. Waterston, Bookseller, 30 Berry St., Liverpool L1, Merseyside, England.

3. *The Netherlands* (*for All European Books*)

Antiquariaat Spinoza, Den Texstraat 26, Amsterdam, Netherlands.

T. Wever, Boekhandel, Franeker, Netherlands.

E. J. Brill, Leiden, Oude Rijn 33a, Netherlands.

Index